s Track, Kills 2 and Injures 12 *July 5, 1950* • Racing on
ar Race Won by Thomas in 6:30.05 *September 4,* ng
to Race at Daytona Beach *January 20, 1952* • Stock Car Races and Girls'
uto Racers Plan Meet: Safety to Be Stressed Oct. 15 at Philadelphia Session
2 • G.M. Show: Stock Car with 210-Horsepower Engine Is One of the New
s 137.01 in Racing Car Event at Daytona Beach *February 13, 1953* • Auto
cord Set: Shaw Drives Average 117.06 MPH at Daytona Beach *January 10,*
Hunted in Daytona Riot *February 27, 1956* • Daytona Beach's New Automobile
ont *October 28, 1956* • Parks Sets Auto Mark: He Drives Experimental Car
Other Florida Locales Have Busy Stock-Car Racing Season *February 10, 1957*
y 20, 1957* • Auto Purse Is Raised: Darlington Offers $53,265 for Labor Day
Fans Will Get Unobstructed View at New Track: High Speed Oval at Daytona
Speedway at Daytona Beach: Racing Car Slips on a Turn After 128-Mile-Per-
Leave Safely *March 30, 1959* • Jerry Unser Dies of Injuries: Stock-Car Race
Noisiest Fans *May 31, 1959* • Roberts Breaks Stock Car Mark: His Average
k as Auto Hits Fence *September 6, 1959* • Tilting All Machines: Sports Car
na Beach Speedway Lures Visitors *November 13, 1960* • Like That Car in a
an Hour *February 7, 1964* • Nascar Approves "Fancy" Engines: High Risers,
Stock-Car Racing *December 14, 1965* • Chrysler to Quit Stock-Car Racing
p. 4 *December 25, 1966* • Firestone Will Offer $750,000 in Prizes to Nascar
ars *February 12, 1969* • Moon Shining Bright on Stock Cars *June 11, 1969*
Auto Manufacturers Keep One Eye on the Track and the Other on Consumer
25, 1970* • Daytona Limits Carburetors to Equalize the Competition *February*
k Auto Racing Buried with Paving of Columbia Track *April 28, 1971* • Racing
alls It a Career *January 12, 1972* • Cheating in Stock Car Racing Is a Way to
pril 21, 1974* • Bammin' and Frammin' Set for Another Healthy Year *January*
sts 200th Victory *July 5, 1984* • Full Speed Ahead for Nascar's Big Hero *May*
Too Dangerous? *May 24, 1987* • Gentlemen, Restrict Your Engines *May 12,*
The Father of Stock-Car Racing *June 8, 1992* • Petty's Career Comes to a
ruary 15, 1994* • Tobacco Law May Stunt Racing's Growth *August 29, 1996*
dergoes Heart Surgery *November 27, 1997* • For Stock Car World's Reigning
Racing and Golf Reach Out to Spectators and Sponsors *June 17, 1999* •
r Figure Keeps Everybody Happy *October 20, 1999* • Lee Petty, 86, Racing
rash *May 13, 2000* • How Stock Cars Became Icons of Americana *May 21,*
r Star Killed on Last Lap of Daytona 500 *February 19, 2001* • Racer's Death
Death, a Rebound for Nascar *March 25, 2001* • Top Drivers Criticize Nascar
001 • Earnhardt Jr. Helps Nascar Find Its Way Back *July 15, 2001* • Panel
ay: Speed Kills *August 22, 2001* • Nascar Drivers Will Use Safety Restraint
01 • Questions Line the Road as Nascar Steers into a New Year *December*
extel to Be Top Sponsor of Nascar's Elite Series *June 18, 2003* • Fan Loyalty
ar Looks Past White Male Roots *January 7, 2004* • Nascar Changes System
ar May Be on Its Way *March 28, 2004* • In Final Ratings, Nascar Wins *June*
smay of Drivers, Nascar Is Slow in Adapting High Tech to Pit Road *September*
Rating for Nascar Final Race *November 23, 2004* • Nascar Seeks Crossover
shaping Nascar *April 17, 2005* • As the Wheel Turns, Nascar Speculation
Road Rage *September 20, 2005* • ESPN and ABC to Take Nascar from
ecember 8, 2005* • When North Meets Nascar *December 11, 2005*

Speed Show

A **New York Times** BOOK

SPEED SHOW

HOW NASCAR WON THE HEART OF AMERICA

DAVE CALDWELL

KINGFISHER
BOSTON

KINGFISHER

a Houghton Mifflin Company imprint
222 Berkeley Street
Boston, Massachusetts 02116
www.houghtonmifflinbooks.com

First published in 2006
2 4 6 8 10 9 7 5 3 1
Printed in China
1TR/0706/PROSP/PICA(PICA)/130MA/C

The type for this book was set in Bembo.
Book design by Nik Keevil, www.keevildesign.co.uk
Cover design by Mike Buckley
Photo consultant: Alison Morley

LIBRARY OF CONGRESS CATALOGING-IN-PUBLICATION DATA

CALDWELL, DAVE.

SPEED SHOW: HOW NASCAR WON THE HEART OF AMERICA / DAVE CALDWELL.

P. CM.

INCLUDES BIBLIOGRAPHICAL REFERENCES AND INDEX.

ISBN-13: 978-0-7534-6011-5

ISBN-10: 0-7534-6011-4

1. STOCK CAR RACING—UNITED STATES—JUVENILE LITERATURE.   2. NASCAR

(ASSOCIATION)—JUVENILE LITERATURE.   I. TITLE.

GV1029.9.S74C35 2006

796.720973—DC22   2006003993

A note on the articles: Throughout this book, excerpts from articles that were published in *The New York Times* appear as sidebars. These excerpts have been modified to fit the format of the book. Source notes to refer the reader to the original articles can be found at the back of the book.

To Ben and Danny, my crew

Contents

ONE

February 18, 2001
"It's What We Do"

The pack of stock cars, their engines growling, had circled the racetrack 199 times. Nearly half the cars still on the track had been crumpled in a spectacular wreck that left skid marks on the pavement. It had been a long, tough race. There was just one more lap—two and a half miles—to go.

The Daytona 500 is the biggest stock car race there is, and about 175,000 people were at the track that sunny Sunday afternoon. Golden sunlight streamed through a window in the crowded media center on the speedway infield. I got out of my chair and stood at a television monitor, ringed by other newspaper reporters, to watch the last lap.

Dale Earnhardt's number 3 Chevy hits the wall at 174 mph on the final lap of the Daytona 500.

Michael Waltrip was going to win the race, and it would be a good story. Waltrip was thirty-seven years old and had never won a Nascar Winston Cup race (the racing series is now called the Nextel Cup). He was going to win for his new boss, the seven-time driving champion Dale Earnhardt. Earnhardt drove a car owned by Richard Childress. But five years earlier he had started his own racing team, made up of cars driven by Waltrip, Steve Park, and his twenty-six-year-old son, Dale Jr., all formidable drivers.

Dale Earnhardt Jr. chased Waltrip around the last turn of the racetrack, but he was too far behind his teammate to catch him. All Waltrip needed to do was cross the finish line. Then he could celebrate the greatest day of his career.

Waltrip's older brother, Darrell, a former Winston Cup champion, was a commentator on the telecast of the race. Darrell had been a chatterbox during his driving career and was still one as an announcer. He admired his younger brother, a tall man with a thatch of wavy brown hair and a quick wit.

The volume of the television was turned up in the media center so we could listen to Darrell. We all expected him to say something poignant or funny.

Suddenly the camera cut away from Waltrip's car. Dale Earnhardt, driving his familiar black Chevrolet with the slanted white number 3 painted on the sides and roof, thumped into the wall, along with a yellow number 36 car driven by Ken Schrader. Several reporters gasped.

Wrecks sometimes unfold on the last laps of races as the drivers make a last bid for extra points in the drivers' standings, not to mention prize money. But it was unusual for Earnhardt to wreck now. He was ensured a good finish, and, besides that, the driver of one of his cars was going to win the race. Earnhardt rarely crashed—he seemed to know just where to poke the nose of his car to gain position while staying out of trouble.

The camera cut back to Michael Waltrip's blue Chevrolet. He had just won his first race. Waltrip had driven in 462 Winston Cup races over the last sixteen years. If nothing else, he was persistent. He took a victory lap, passing the accident scene, parked his car in Victory Lane, and pulled himself out of its window, celebrating like almost every other winner of a race—by raising his fists and whooping. The fans in the stands roared right along with him.

Darrell Waltrip hollered over the airwaves: "Man, my daddy would be so happy!"

Such is the appeal of Nascar, short for the National Association for Stock Car Auto Racing. Nascar is everywhere, on television sets in living rooms and dens, because millions of people love it with a passion. It is probably best known for its top racing series, now called the Nextel Cup, which travels from racetrack to racetrack during a demanding thirty-six-race schedule.

Michael Waltrip with his daughter after a 2003 win at Talladega.

The infield media center is a good place for reporters to cover a race, because it's near the garages. After a race, every driver must drive his car to the garage area so his crew can put the car on its tractor-trailer to take it back to the team's shop. The winner of the Daytona 500 holds a news conference in the press box above the tall grandstands, but reporters can interview other drivers in the infield after the race. I wanted to interview Dale Earnhardt, to get his reaction to Waltrip's victory. Earnhardt was not a driver who liked to hang around the track, especially after races he did not win. So after Waltrip crossed the finish line, I walked quickly to Earnhardt's tractor-trailer and waited for him.

Earnhardt was stock car racing's biggest star—fans loved or hated him. He had won seventy-six races and nearly $42 million as a stock car driver on the Winston Cup series, but his success was only one of the reasons why fans felt so strongly about him. There was something old-fashioned about Dale. He was a millionaire, but he still seemed rough around the edges.

Dale Earnhardt poses moments before the 2001 Daytona 500.

Dale Earnhardt grew up in Kannapolis, North Carolina, a town with a big mill where they made sheets and towels. His father, Ralph, also raced cars, but he was not as good as his son would become. Fans loved Dale's black car and his brash style. They especially loved it when he beat Jeff Gordon, a clean-cut driver from Indiana who was twenty years younger than Earnhardt and had won three championships in the 1990s.

I expected Earnhardt to amble through the garage area at any moment. His accident had not looked serious. He and Schrader had appeared to bounce off the wall rather than plow into it. Earnhardt wore a white driving suit, and he always pulled on a black or white baseball cap and wraparound sunglasses after a race. I imagined he would smile through his mustache, which was thick and bushy like a push broom. Maybe he hadn't won, but one of his drivers had.

I had talked to Earnhardt two days before the race as he sat on a golf cart outside his mobile home. Nascar officials had made some rule changes about the aerodynamics of the cars, which they thought would make the Daytona 500 more exciting. The officials decided that the best way to ensure closer racing, with more competition for the lead, was actually to slow the cars down. One of the major changes was to require the installation of a strip of sheet metal, called a "blade," on the roof of the car, just behind the windshield. The blade would create more wind resistance and make the cars go slower. During two qualifying races three days before the Daytona 500, the field stayed clumped together and there were, indeed, more lead changes. Earnhardt liked Nascar's solutions.

"I want to be driving racecars to race them," he said.

As I waited for him after the race, I thought he'd be pleased. Earnhardt was just about the only person who had believed in Michael Waltrip, who had

Earnhardt with Dale Jr., who also became a huge presence in the sport.

struggled for recognition from teams that were not as good as this one. I thought Earnhardt might needle some people about that.

Ten minutes became twenty, then thirty. Earnhardt's crew silently gathered all of his equipment and began to load it onto the truck. Earnhardt and his car hadn't arrived. I realized he must have been hurt worse than I had thought. Maybe he was at the hospital.

Aftermath: A tarp is placed over Dale Earnhardt's car.

I had to return to the media center to write my story about the race for the next day's *New York Times*. The audio from the postrace interview was piped into the media center. As I listened to Michael Waltrip, he sounded uncharacteristically subdued after the race. He was disappointed because Earnhardt did not stop by Victory Lane to playfully grab him by the back of the neck and give him a bear hug. Waltrip sounded as if he wanted to give Earnhardt a bear hug, too.

"The only reason I won this race," Waltrip said, "was because of Dale Earnhardt."

I opened my laptop and started writing. Time passed with no word on Earnhardt. Maybe it was just my imagination, but the room seemed to get quieter with each passing minute. No news, in this case, was definitely not good news. I overheard another reporter make a call on his cell phone. He spoke in a whisper.

"They said it was instant," he said.

Instant? Did that mean what I thought it meant? Did Earnhardt die instantly? I stopped writing for a moment. More whispers came from other people around the room: Nascar was going to make an announcement at seven p.m.

I called my editors to let them know what I was hearing. Another *Times* reporter, Robert Lipsyte, who was seated in the press box, had done the same thing. Waltrip's victory was becoming an afterthought. Had Dale Earnhardt really been killed?

Earnhardt's pit crew hurries to get number 3 back on the track during a race in 1991.

It seemed impossible to me. Not only was Earnhardt a champion driver, but he also seemed indestructible. Sometimes he used his car to nudge other drivers out of his way. He drove hard enough to have earned the nickname "the Intimidator."

No way was Dale Earnhardt dead.

In the moments after Dale Earnhardt hit the wall, a voice in his headset, crackling with static and rising concern, said: "You okay, Dale? Talk to us, talk to us."

But there was no answer. Crumpled in his famed number 3 black Goodwrench Chevrolet, the Intimidator, bleeding from his ears, nose, and mouth, was probably already dead. As red tow trucks and white ambulances swarmed around the black car, the voice on Earnhardt's radio frequency, also heard by thousands at the track with race radios, seemed to quiver with panic. "Talk to us, Dale."

His death left a hole in the heart of a sport as close and insular as a traveling carnival.

At seven o'clock, Mike Helton, who had become the president of Nascar the previous November, lumbered into the media center. Dozens of television cameramen trailed him. Helton, a big man with dark wavy hair and a thick mustache, picked up a microphone and looked sadly at the reporters in the packed media center. He seemed to be gazing at something far away before composing himself. He began to speak slowly.

"This is undoubtedly one of the toughest announcements I've ever personally had to make," Helton said slowly. "After the accident in turn four at the end of the Daytona 500, we've lost Dale Earnhardt."

Lost. Helton's announcement jolted me. I'd covered auto racing for more than ten years, and I had seen my share of serious accidents, but no one had died in a race I covered. And this was not just any driver who had been killed: this was the reigning icon of the sport.

Helton seemed to be saying that the sport had lost much more than a great competitor. He was reminding us that auto racing is extremely dangerous. Even its toughest celebrity was not immune to the risks.

Earnhardt was killed instantly when his car hit the wall, a doctor said. He was taken to a hospital, where he was soon pronounced dead. By the time his death was announced, the speedway had all but emptied. After the press conference, I called my editor again to find out my assignment. *The Times* would run three stories the next day. Bob Lipsyte would write a news story for the front page of the paper. I'd been writing for *The Times* for less than a year, but I knew auto-racing stories rarely made the front page.

A wall honoring Earnhardt was put up in his hometown of Kannapolis, North Carolina.

I would write about how the sweetest moment of Waltrip's career had been overwhelmed by the news of Earnhardt's death. Then the editors said they wanted me to write Dale Earnhardt's obituary. It was a hard story to write. He was only forty-nine years old.

For the next few hours, I wrote faster than I ever had before. At eleven-thirty, I left the media center, which was still filled with reporters, feeling exhausted.

• • •

When I headed back to the racetrack early the next morning, it seemed like a completely different place. Daytona International Speedway had been all but deserted when I left Sunday night. Monday morning, there was a traffic jam. It seemed everyone who was still in town wanted to pay tribute to Earnhardt.

There is a big fountain outside the racetrack with a statue of Bill and Mary France, the founder of Nascar and his wife, at the center. Earnhardt's fans had come early and set memorials to him around the fountain.

Fans of all ages gathered to pay tribute after the fatal crash.

There were flowers, Earnhardt T-shirts, posters, and signs, many handmade and most including poetry. A man from New Jersey told me he had delayed his trip home so he could place a poem at the makeshift shrine.

The race fan's eleven-year-old daughter had written the poem the night before. She had called him from New Jersey and read it to him over the phone. The next morning, he went to a drugstore near the track and bought a big sheet of white poster board and a marker. He wrote down her poem, part of which read, "He died doing what he liked best. Now it is time for our hero to rest," and taped it to the fountain.

There would be a candlelight vigil later that night at the racetrack, during which people would offer prayers for Earnhardt and his family. But many fans did not want to wait until then.

By lunchtime, the area around the fountain was crowded. Hundreds ringed the memorial, and many of them prayed. People in Daytona Beach bought up every souvenir with Earnhardt's name or picture.

A woman strode toward the fountain as if it were the altar in a church and dramatically dropped to one knee to say a prayer. A family formed a circle, held hands, and prayed. A boy in the circle sneaked a peek at the Earnhardt shrine.

I don't think Earnhardt was all that religious. In fact, I think people liked him because he was rough around the edges. He hadn't exactly grown up in a poor household, but he had only an eighth-grade education and had fought his way to the top.

Late that afternoon, a news conference was held in a big white tent at the speedway. Helton walked in and said there would still be a race the following Sunday in Rockingham, North Carolina. Earnhardt's car had been taken to a secret place and was being examined for clues that might show what had caused the fatal accident.

Officials already knew that Earnhardt had died of head injuries, particularly to the base of his brain. Dr. Steve Bohannon, the director of medical services at the speedway, was then asked if a support collar known as a HANS device might have saved Earnhardt's life.

Bohannon said he could not answer. HANS (short for "head and neck support") devices were relatively new. The HANS device is a collar that fits over the back of the driver's head and collarbone and attaches to the seat. Tethers connecting the helmet to the device are designed to keep the driver's head and neck upright if the car is in a collision or stops suddenly. Earnhardt hadn't liked newfangled things. He didn't even wear a full face helmet when he drove—just a pair of black goggles that made him look more intimidating.

The news conference was televised on cable news channels and the tent, packed with equipment and reporters, looked like a television studio. I remember thinking that was unusual. Earnhardt was the most famous stock car driver there was, but until he arrived on the scene, stock car racing had not been such a big deal.

The HANS helmet has a support collar that keeps the head stable in a crash.

But things had changed overnight.

Nascar was rapidly developing national appeal. The 2001 season was the first in which most races would be shown on two big television networks, Fox and NBC. It would also be the first in which Nascar races were held at big new racetracks outside Chicago and Kansas City, two Midwestern cities that had not previously been part of Nascar's turf.

Three years later fans at the 2004 Daytona 500 still remember.

I was assigned to cover the race in Rockingham, where I arrived on a damp and foggy Friday morning. A tent had been set up for another news conference. Nascar officials said they had looked at the wreckage of Earnhardt's car. His seat belt was broken. He might have lived if it had not snapped.

Richard Childress grimly said that a driver had been selected to replace Earnhardt for this race and for the foreseeable future.

Kevin Harvick was twenty-five, but looked as if he had just graduated from high school. Childress said Harvick could handle the pressure of driving the car that was intended for Earnhardt.

Harvick's main sponsor would be G. M. Goodwrench, as Earnhardt's had been, but Childress decided to put Harvick in a car that was painted white instead of black and carried the number 29 instead of Earnhardt's famous number 3. Childress knew Harvick could handle only so much pressure.

Then Michael Waltrip stepped up to the microphone and said he would test the HANS device but not wear it in the next race. Dale Earnhardt Jr. was at the news conference, too, speaking publicly for the first time since his father's death.

Dale Jr., who had joined the Winston Cup series as a full-time driver only the year before, had attended his father's funeral that Wednesday and a memorial service in Charlotte the day before the race.

Sterling Marlin, a veteran driver, had been blamed by some race fans for causing the crash. Marlin had tapped Dale Earnhardt Sr.'s car in a way that it caused a spin. Dale Jr. said pointedly at the news conference that the crash was not Marlin's fault.

With the help of Dale Jr., Nascar was slowly moving away from the accident. The drivers had lost one of their own, a driver they admired and liked, but they seemed determined to move on. The other driver who had been involved in the accident, Ken Schrader, would be driving a new yellow car in the race at Rockingham. He talked briefly in the garage area about the accident a week earlier, but he seemed to want to concentrate on the race ahead.

Kevin Harvick replaced Earnhardt and Nascar tried to move on.

It seemed strange to me that Schrader wanted to race so soon after a terribly costly wreck. "It's what we do," he said solemnly.

Still, the memory of Earnhardt's death was everywhere. Every car in the race bore a little sticker with the number 3 on it. Many crew members wore black caps with number 3s, even if they were not from Earnhardt's crew.

Dale Earnhardt won six of his seven titles while driving the number 3 Chevrolet for Richard Childress Racing, immortalizing his number in the hearts of devoted fans. Number 3 is everywhere. It is on hats, T-shirts, and bumper stickers.

But what is sacred to many fans is not sacred to Nascar, which owns all numbers and assigns them to teams each year for a fee. Nascar does not retire numbers.

It is one of the few traditions Nascar has followed. There have been no exceptions, not even when Richard Petty, known as the King, retired after 1992. Petty won seven titles and two hundred races—more victories than any other driver—in his five-decade career.

But each season Petty still sends a $2,000 check to Nascar for an owner's license. He has to be assigned the number 43 because teams keep their numbers each year as long as they continue to run them. Since Petty's retirement, Wally Dallenbach Jr., John Andretti, Bobby Hamilton, Christian Fittipaldi, and now Jeff Green have raced in the number 43 car.

Unlike Petty, Childress has withheld the number 3 from competition in the Cup series since Earnhardt's death. Childress said he still paid Nascar each year for the owner's license and held the rights to the number 3 design that was on the Earnhardt racecar.

So what will become of the number 3? Will it race again? Should it race again?

Some say yes, some no.

The most intriguing answer came from Childress in 2005: "Never say never."

Darrell Waltrip and his wife, Stevie, led a prayer over the public-address system, and the race began. On the very first lap, Ron Hornaday hit Dale Earnhardt Jr.'s car from behind. Earnhardt's bright red Chevrolet with the tilting number 8s smacked the turn three wall. One wrecked car tends to collect other cars that are trying to get out of the way. Cars began to swerve, then spin like pinwheels, sending thick plumes of tire smoke into the air. Besides Hornaday's and Earnhardt's, five other cars were also involved in the accident.

The crash looked similar to the one that had killed Dale Sr. a week earlier. The front of Dale Jr.'s car was pushed almost all the way in, too battered to continue. The crowd stood, and it seemed as if every fan's neck was craned toward turn three to see how bad the accident was. But Earnhardt quickly climbed from the car and said he was fine. He promised he would race the following week in Las Vegas.

Workers took nearly a half-hour to clear debris from the track. Then it began to rain and the race was stopped. It would be completed the next day. A week that had already been long and lousy seemed as if it would never end.

Dale Earnhardt Jr.'s car one week after his father's fatal crash.

That Monday, February 26, was bright and sunny, but Nascar races that are run on Mondays are not as exciting as weekend races. Most of the fans have gone back to work. When the race resumed at eleven a.m., there were wide gaps of empty seats in the aluminum grandstands.

Jeff Gordon, Dale Earnhardt Sr.'s rival, started the race in the pole position and led with fifty laps left. Then he lost the lead to a yellow Chevrolet with tilting red number 1s on the top and sides. Behind the wheel was Steve Park.

Park was thirty-three years old and from Long Island—not one of the drivers who had grown up in the Southeast. But the owner of a Winston Cup team had watched Park drive in smaller races and liked what he saw. The owner's name was Dale Earnhardt Sr.

Bobby Labonte tried to pass Park several times in the last five laps. Once, their cars brushed each other, but both drove on, and Park won the race. He spun his car around so the driver's-side window faced the grandstands, and then he reached toward his gearshift.

Steve Park waves a black cap on his victory lap at Rockingham.

Park had snapped a baseball cap around the base of the gearshift. It was black, with a white number 3 on the front. Park held it out the window and waved it at the fans. He said later that he was crying as he took his victory lap.

Park had driven in ninety-one Winston Cup races before Rockingham and had won only once. But Earnhardt, who saw talent other car owners might not have, had given Park the same chance he had given Michael Waltrip. That Monday in Rockingham was emotional, but the emotions were far different from the ones eight days earlier. Another race had been run, and everyone was relieved. Jeff Gordon said that Park's victory was almost as good as if Dale Earnhardt Jr. had won.

Gordon won the following weekend in Las Vegas, and Harvick, who permanently replaced Dale Earnhardt Sr., won the week after that in Atlanta. Gordon won his fourth Winston Cup championship. The stock car racing world tilted back on its axis.

Nascar had not been ruined by Earnhardt's death. Before the accident on turn four of the Daytona 500, Nascar had been well on its way to becoming a phenomenon, but it was Dale Earnardt's accident that had pushed the sport further into the jet stream of the American consciousness. In fact, more people than ever started paying attention to the Winston Cup series. Dale Earnhardt would have smiled through his push-broom mustache at that.

TWO

The Basics
"Anybody's a Threat"

Talladega Superspeedway, the big Nascar racetrack in eastern Alabama, unfolds before your eyes as you approach on Interstate 20. You round a stand of trees and the tall multicolored grandstands loom to the right, waiting to be filled.

But on a race weekend, it's not the tall grandstands or even the massive oval track that inspire the most awe—it's the excitement and the fans that fill them. The track was built on flat ground that used to be a soybean farm. When Nascar pays a visit, it seems as if every inch of that ground is covered by tents, vans, and RVs, even if rain has turned the fields to mud. Many of the campers cook hamburgers and hot dogs over fires, and a thick cloud of pungent wood smoke hangs over the track.

Talladega is the biggest and fastest track in the Nextel Cup series. The thousands of campers outside the track can make it seem crowded and overwhelming. But those who find a parking spot and hang out for a while usually find Talladega to be a place they visit again.

There is much more to a stock car race than just the race itself. It is a spectacle, like a state or county fair, or an outdoor rock concert. People come and stay awhile, usually from Friday night to Sunday night.

And there is plenty to do. Many race fans become friends over weekends spent together year after year. There are often concerts in the infield of the bigger ovals. Some speedways, such as Talladega, have smaller tracks nearby that host smaller races.

An area outside the track is turned into a midway, with food, most of it not very healthy, and entertainment, usually country-western bands. And there are tractor-trailers, one side open, from which all kinds of merchandise are sold.

The most popular drivers—Dale Earnhardt Jr., Tony Stewart, and Jeff Gordon—have their own souvenir trucks, and teammates on lesser-known teams pool their resources to sell their goods. The drivers receive a portion of the money from the sales of souvenirs such as baseball caps, bobble-head dolls, T-shirts, and one of the most popular items, tiny die-cast metal replicas of the racecars.

Talladega Superspeedway is long and it is wide. Think rush-hour traffic, except everybody is pressing the accelerator as if living beyond the moment is not a priority. "Talladega is the most nerve-racking experience that you can go through as a driver," said Tony Stewart in 2000. "The concrete wall was about a foot away from me and the guy on the inside of me was about three or four inches away from me. I can only imagine what the middle two guys felt like. You've got guys behind you. You've got cars in front of you. You've got cars beside you, and you're running 195 miles an hour."

Actually, Stewart was exaggerating. Chances are, the pack was going only between 175 and 185 miles per hour. "You just can't seem to get settled down and get in a rhythm," he said. "It's not about what you and your car can do. It's about what everybody else is doing to you and your car."

Every year Talladega hosts two Nextel Cup races, and each draws an estimated 155,000 fans. The traffic jams before and after the races are immense. So are the television audiences. But although fans who watch races on television have faster access to replays, those who come to a race have a more complete experience.

A race is often referred to as "The Show" because, like a Broadway musical, it affects all the senses. Sunday-afternoon sunshine brightens the colors on the cars, which usually carry the colors and logos of corporate sponsors. When races are run at night, tall poles covered in lights illuminate the track and reflect off the cars so that they seem to glitter as they hurtle around the track. Sometimes they trail orange-yellow sparks.

Exhaust from cars dissipates quickly, but the pungent smell of burned fuel and tires lingers. And the noise is deafening. The roar of so many cars grinding around a track a couple of times, let alone two hundred or four hundred times, can have an overwhelming effect.

The minutes before any race are filled with anticipation. At most tracks, "The Star-Spangled Banner" is sung by a well-known recording artist, and a flyover of military jets, planes, or helicopters follows.

Then another celebrity steps to the microphone and hollers, "Gentlemen, start your engines!"

The crowd roars as the cars begin to grumble and then lurch around the track to warm up.

In a Nextel Cup race there are almost always forty-three cars, which align in rows of two behind a pace car, usually a sports car, as they take their warm-up laps. The starting order is determined by qualifying runs earlier in the weekend, or, if qualifying runs are rained out, by the points standings. The fastest qualifier earns the "pole position," so named because his car's number is atop the tall scoring pole at the start-finish line.

An electronic signpost lists laps completed at the top, and the leading cars in order.

Even though the qualifying runs are meant to weed out slower drivers, Nascar has put in place rules that all but guarantee that the series regulars will make the starting field, even if they qualify poorly. The regulars are who the fans come to see—most have a favorite driver. Even though it's difficult to see the drivers' faces behind the windshields, they become known by their cars.

After a few warm-up laps, the pace car pulls off the track and the driver with pole position slows down just enough to bunch up the field behind him. He watches for the flagman stationed on a stand at the start-finish line outside the track to wave a green flag. Then the driver stomps on the gas pedal, the fans stand and roar, and the race is under way.

George W. Bush, then the governor of Texas, waves the starting flag at the Primestar 500 in 1999.

The basic rules are simple: each race is set for a certain distance and a certain number of laps. The first driver to cross the finish line wins.

Usually the forty-three cars blend into chaotic, blinding, noisy packs as the race develops, but technology has made the competitors surprisingly easy to follow. Sensors are built into the front of each car to keep track of its position and speed.

Changes in position are reflected in a tall

pole and on scoreboards positioned near most grandstands. There are giant television monitors so that fans who miss a challenge for the lead can see a replay.

The cars whirl around the banked track, and sometimes many laps pass without a change in standing. At times the leader will pull away, but most of the cars remain tightly packed. Because of Nascar's often-changing rule book, most of the cars are closely matched. But it is in a driver's best interest to stay just ahead of or just behind another driver.

Aerodynamics play a critical role. Two cars traveling nose to tail can actually go faster than a single car. The front car slices through the air, enabling the second to encounter less resistance. At the same time, the second car changes the aerodynamics behind the first, reducing the amount of drag at the back of the lead vehicle. The tactic is called "drafting."

Drafting: The front car slices through the air, reducing the resistance encountered by the second car.

Many cars "join the draft" early in a race, resulting in what announcers call a freight train. Late in a close race, crew chiefs whose drivers are teammates or who drive cars made by the same manufacturer will form a draft to pass other contenders.

Perhaps the most common misconception of the popularity of Nascar is that most people go to races because they like to watch the cars crash. A smoky, fiery wreck does cause the fans to rise from their seats, but a racetrack is far bigger than a football or baseball stadium, and the action occurs all over the track, not just at one point. Many wrecks take place far away from a fan's vantage point. They also end quickly, usually within seconds. By the time most fans spot a crash and focus on it with binoculars, safety crews have arrived on the scene and the drivers, in most cases, have pulled themselves out of their cars. Often a driver involved in an accident will wave, as if to signal that he or she is okay. That gesture usually draws a roar of approval from the crowd. Not many fans want drivers to get injured, because, after all, the drivers are a big part of The Show.

When the flagman spots an accident, he waves a yellow flag, signaling a caution period. Tow trucks haul away the wrecked cars and workers clean up any debris. Sometimes they have to put a special resin on the track to soak up spilled oil or gasoline. A piece of debris falling off a car can also cause a caution period, which drivers can detect by lights posted on the walls and atop the scoreboard.

Particularly serious accidents will lead to a red flag. The drivers are required to stop in a line, turn off their engines, and wait until the accident scene is cleared.

What fans really like to see is close, hard racing. Nothing stirs the crowd more than a lead change, particularly if it involves a popular driver. Dale Earnhardt Sr. was practically worshiped every time he drove at Talladega, where he won ten Winston Cup races—far more than any other driver.

After Earnhardt's death, the crowd at Talladega adopted Dale Jr. as their favorite. When he took the lead late in a race in May 2005, the fans near the start–finish line stood and cheered loudly.

Dale Jarrett scrambles out of his burning car at the Pocono track in 2003.

Dale Earnhardt Jr.'s racing career began long before he slipped into a racecar as a teenager.

It started with two families, the Earnhardts and the Eurys, who lived in Kannapolis, North Carolina, in the 1960s.

Today they are one family, intertwined over the decades by marriage and friendship. Tony Eury Sr. is the crew chief of Dale Jr.'s number 8 racecar, and he is also his uncle. And the car chief is Tony Eury Jr., Earnhardt's cousin.

"It's a lot more family than it is professional, which I like," Earnhardt said in 2004.

That family began as a friendship between Ralph Earnhardt and Ralph Eury, who were racecar drivers in the 1960s, mostly in the lower tiers of the sport. Eury made his living as a plumber and the two became friends, the story goes, when Eury went to Earnhardt's house to do some work. They started talking about racing, and the relationship was forged. Earnhardt built engines for Eury's cars.

Eury Sr. eventually became a crew chief for Dale Earnhardt's Busch series team. When Earnhardt went in search of a driver for that team, he asked Eury for advice.

"Dale Sr. came to me in 1997 and asked me, did I think I could make a racecar driver out of Dale Jr.?" Eury said. "I said, 'I don't know but we can try.' At that time, we didn't know whether he was going to make a driver or not. My comment to him was 'Why spend your money on somebody else's kid when you can spend it on your own?' I said, 'Let's go for it.'" When Earnhardt Jr. was a rookie in 2000, he frequently clashed with Eury Jr. In 2003, there was talk that Eury Jr. might leave the team.

But it is not as easy to walk away from family.

In the end, no one really wanted to make that change. In 2005, Eury Jr., who has spent years under his father's tutelage, became Dale Jr.'s crew chief.

Dale Jr. lost that lead to Jeff Gordon, who won the race. But that cheer, which was as loud as the engines of the cars themselves, demonstrated how fans feel about their favorite stars.

Not surprisingly, given the large fan base and commercial tie-ins, the prize money at Nascar events is huge. Mike Waltrip won more than $1.3 million the day Dale Earnhardt was killed. Even at smaller Nextel Cup tracks a winner receives a check for more than $150,000. That prize money, called the purse, goes to the car's owners, but the driver gets a percentage of the win. Exactly how much is determined by the driver's contract with his sponsor.

There is also a championship on the line. From 1971 to 2003, drivers raced for the Winston Cup, which was sponsored by the R. J. Reynolds Tobacco Company. Then the sponsorship was taken over by Nextel, a communications corporation.

Jeff Gordon

Jimmie Johnson

Since 1949, the first full season of Nascar racing, two drivers have won seven championships: Richard Petty, the perpetually smiling driver nicknamed "the King," and Dale Earnhardt Sr., "the Intimidator," who won his last championship in 1994. Jeff Gordon won four Winston Cup championships from 1995 to 2001, and it looked as if he would need only a few more years to match the King and the Intimidator. But a new group of talented drivers came along: Matt Kenseth won a championship, then Tony Stewart, then Kurt Busch, then Stewart again. Gordon's teammate, Jimmie Johnson, became just as formidable a driver as Gordon.

The door to the most exclusive club in Nascar opens only about once or twice a decade, on the rare occasion when a driver wins multiple championship titles. Of all the competitors who have raced in Nascar's premier division since the sport was organized in 1949, only fourteen have managed to win more than one title in their careers. The last time someone joined the list of multiple winners was 2005, when Tony Stewart took his second title.

"It's a big deal to win a championship, but it's a huge deal when you start winning more than one," Jeff Gordon said before Stewart's win. "You go into one class when you win a championship, you go to a whole other one after you start winning more than one.

"I think it definitely separates you, really, from a lot of the other drivers when you do that."

In Nascar history, two drivers have won seven championships, and twelve have won at least two:

Seven	Richard Petty, Dale Earnhardt
Four	Jeff Gordon
Three	Lee Petty, Darrell Waltrip, Cale Yarborough, David Pearson
Two	Terry Labonte, Ned Jarrett, Joe Weatherly, Buck Baker, Tim Flock, Herb Thomas, Tony Stewart

It is often said that every stock car race is really two: one to win the race itself, and one for the championship. Nascar uses a championship points system that seems complicated and unwieldy—but it has withstood the test of time with a few modifications.

The system is the same for each race, no matter its significance or prize money. The winner receives 180 points and second place is worth 170 points. The next finishers each receive five points fewer than the place before them: third place gets 165; fourth place, 160; fifth place, 155, and sixth, 150. After that, the points awarded per place decrease by 4 points from seventh to eleventh and 3 points from twelfth to forty-third. The driver in last place receives 34 points. In addition, drivers receive 5 points for each lap they lead. The driver who leads the most laps gets another 5 points on top of the bonuses for the laps led.

At Nascar's request, an easygoing man named Bob Latford created the scoring system in 1975. Before that, it had been even more complicated: Richard Petty won the 1974 championship with 5,037.75 points. Latford, a racing historian and public relations man with a handlebar mustache, did some doodling on a napkin, the story goes, until he came up with a method that rewarded drivers who consistently did well rather than drivers who drove spectacularly one week and not so well the next.

Richard Petty celebrates his 1973 championship win with his daughter on his shoulder.

Latford, in retrospect, seems like a genius. His point system made for close competition: between 1975 and 2003, when Latford's system was tweaked to give the winner of a race 5 more points, eleven championship races were decided by fewer than 50 points—the difference between first and twelfth places in a single race.

Rusty Wallace beat Dale Earnhardt by 12 points for the 1989 championship, and Alan Kulwicki won the 1992 championship over Bill Elliott by 10 points. There were some runaways, as in 1994, when Earnhardt beat Mark Martin by 444 points, but the championship chase usually lasted until the final race of the season, making every race meaningful.

In 2004 the system was altered again and the season was divided into two parts. After twenty-six races, the top ten drivers are separated from the others and entered in a ten-race "Chase for the Nascar Nextel Cup." Before the first race of the Chase, the driver who has accumulated the most points in the first part of the season receives 5,050 points, the next, 5,045; the next, 5,040, and so on.

At first the drivers were not sure how they felt about this change. Most of them disliked the idea of pushing hard to gain points in the first twenty-six races of the season only to have their lead all but erased before the last ten races.

In 2004, Jeff Gordon had a 293-point lead over Kurt Busch, the seventh-place driver entering the Chase. Gordon's lead over Busch was dropped to 30 points, and at the end of the ten-race series Gordon finished 16 points behind Busch. Afterward, the drivers begrudgingly admitted that the new system had made every lap count.

During the 2005 Chase, Jimmie Johnson said of the other nine drivers, "I truly believe that anybody's a threat."

All of the variables create uncertainty, making many races dramatic until the very end. Dale Earnhardt Sr. lost the Daytona 500 in 1990 to Derrike Cope when one of his tires went flat with only a mile to go. A race is loud, long, and smoky, but it's never over until the flagman at the start-finish line waves a checkered flag.

Eight years later, Earnhardt won the Daytona 500 for the first time. Earnhardt had won plenty of other races at the track, but not the most famous race on the Nascar schedule. He whooped over his car radio on his victory lap, and the crowd whooped along with him.

Nascar's scoring system rewards consistently strong finishes over occasional victories.

THREE
Technology
"Boogity, Boogity, Boogity!"

Like football or baseball or basketball, auto racing is a competition. But unlike, say, a football team, which plays half of its games at a home stadium, Nascar travels from one racetrack to another. A race is more like a three-ring circus that comes to town once or twice a year than a typical sporting event.

There is also more of a mystery in who will win a Nascar race. A football or baseball game pits two teams against each other, but any one of a group of about twenty drivers in the forty-three-car field has a good chance to win a Nextel Cup race. Like any team sport, winning a Nascar race requires group effort and leadership.

Behind every driver there is a crew that maintains the car. The crews are in constant contact with the drivers, making sure that the car runs at top performance throughout the race. Headsets are usually available for rent so a fan can tune into the radio frequencies used by the head of a race team, called the crew chief, to contact the driver. Crew chiefs are a little bit like football coaches; they do not actually perform, but they try to use technology and develop strategies for their drivers.

From atop the grandstand, spotters keep close tabs on their car and driver.

They sit atop "war wagons" at the pits with their laptops, which store detailed information about their cars and the race. Some crew chiefs are as colorful as the drivers. For many years, the crew chief for the driver Ricky Rudd was an enormous man with a thick southern accent and a disarming down-home demeanor. His name was Michael McSwain, but he was better known by competitors and fans alike as "Fatback."

On many weekends during Nascar's Nextel Cup season, the racecar to watch is the number 48 Lowe's Chevrolet driven by Jimmie Johnson. But the star is not always Johnson.

Often, the eyes are on the car.

His crew chief, Chad Knaus, has won fans and made enemies with an approach to Cup competition that is viewed as either innovative or over the line.

A crew chief prepares his car and his team for competition each week. In Nascar, it is not as simple as souping up the engine. Racecars must meet certain standards set down in the rule book each year, from the threads of a screw to the height of a rear quarter-panel. Every car is inspected before each race, and some are inspected again after races.

Knaus sees it as his duty to seek out any and every adjustment that is not expressly forbidden.

"When Nascar hands us that book at the beginning of the year and says, 'Okay, these are the parameters in which you've got to work,' you've got to work every angle in that rule book," Knaus said, adding, "If you don't try to find an advantage, you won't be successful."

Drivers are usually the spokesmen for their race teams. They get to hoist the trophy and are interviewed on television after winning a race. But a victory is very much a team effort. Crew members and technicians prepare a car to run fast, and they keep it running its best during the race.

Members of a crew dress for a race in bright fire-retardant suits similar to those worn by drivers—even with the sponsor's name splashed on the back. In recent years, crew members' names have been sewn on the uniforms, like the names on football jerseys. The entire crew usually participates in the celebration in Victory Lane, an area near the start-finish line. Crew members also participate in what is called a "hat dance," wearing baseball caps with various sponsors' logos and posing for photographs.

"It's all of our responsibility," said Jeff Gordon. "As a driver, my responsibility is to give information to the team about the car and what it's doing, how to make it better, how to start the race the way we should. You know, there's no way to point fingers at any one person. It's a group effort whether you win the race or finish dead last."

Tony Stewart's pit crew celebrates a win at Watkins Glen.

Stock car drivers and their crews have become, in the truest sense, more athletic as racing has gained popularity and the stakes have become higher. Many drivers work out regularly so they can withstand the heat inside the car—which can reach well over 100 degrees—and concentrate on the traffic around them. Races can last as long as four hours, and focusing on the road in the midst of the vibrations and noise of the car can be a real test of endurance. Drivers expend a lot of energy, and they are red-faced and sweaty after races.

Crew members must be in good shape to service the car quickly during a pit stop. They hurdle over the pit walls and back, moving efficiently to save every second: the outcome of a race can be determined by the speed of one of the many pit stops for fuel and fresh tires.

What sets stock car racing apart from sports like baseball or football is the amount of technology involved. Races truly are battles of men and machines.

When Nascar was founded, the idea was for the drivers to use racecars that could be found in any automobile showroom. The word stock meant just that—the cars were taken from the auto dealers' regular inventory, or "stock." Nowadays, the similarities between a racecar and a regular passenger car pretty much end with the shell. A Nextel Cup car is a stripped-down, revved-up version of a passenger automobile. It weighs about 3,500 pounds, about as much as a passenger car, but it does not have much inside except for a well-protected driver's seat, a steering wheel, a gearshift, and the controls needed to drive the car and keep the driver cool. There is no sound system and no glove compartment. The cars don't even have doors—the driver slides through the window, then buttons a thick net over the opening. There is no trunk, no turn signals, and no headlights. Decals of head and taillights are placed on the cars' front and back bumpers to make them look like passenger cars.

What stock cars *do* have is speed. Nextel Cup cars are powered by eight-cylinder engines instead of the four-cylinder engines found in most passenger cars. Stock car engines can generate more than 850 horsepower and a top speed of two hundred miles an hour.

They run on leaded, ultrapremium gasoline. This 112-octane fuel is manufactured by Sunoco and is not available outside the racetrack. It is also more than twice as expensive as the high-test 93-octane gasoline sold at a gas station.

The key to winning is meticulous preparation. The idea is to arrive at a racetrack, push the car off the hauler, fire it up, and have it run fast laps from the first practice session and throughout the weekend. It can be done. But there is much work involved. It is a collective effort among the more than one hundred employees on the top race teams, and no detail seems too small.

Where's the CD player?
The dashboard of a racecar is a far cry from the family sedan's.

1. Tachometer
2. Shift light indicator
3. Water gauge
4. Oil temperature
5. Fuel and oil pressure
6. Battery gauge

Take just one tire used by a race team as an example. Stacks of tires, usually in groups of four, can often be found outside a race team's hauler, the big tractor-trailer that transports the cars and equipment to races. Passenger tires have treads that help the car gain traction on different road surfaces and conditions, but racing tires are completely smooth. The lack of tread makes tires unreliable on icy or wet pavement, which is why races are never held in the rain, but on a dry racetrack the extra surface area allows the cars more traction.

A crew does not just slap any tire on a car when it needs one. Each Goodyear Eagle racing tire is covered with dozens of markings made by the team. Chalk marks denote which tire belongs on a particular wheel—the left or the right side, front or back, and whether the tire is good to use.

There is a sticker with a serial number on the tread of every

Using a blowtorch, a crew member checks tires for pits caused by wear.

unused tire, so the teams and Goodyear can monitor the quality of the tires. Along the face of the tire are tiny numbers written in blue crayon. The tire has been inventoried so that the team can use it for a specific run, even if it is just to qualify for a race. Tire pressures can vary depending on the surface, length, and banking of a racetrack, and crews want to make sure they have differently inflated tires on hand for specific situations.

Literally thousands of variables can go right or wrong during a stock car race. A team must put together a car that is not only capable of going fast, but also durable enough to run at high speeds for hours. On April 30, 1987, Bill Elliott qualified for a race at Talladega by turning a lap at 212.809 miles an hour. Put another way, Elliott drove more than two and a half miles in forty-five seconds. It is a record that still stands, and for a reason. Such high speeds can be a mixed blessing. They are exciting, but can result in serious accidents.

Beginning in 1989, Nascar mandated that restrictor plates be used in the engines when races were held at Talladega and Daytona, its two fastest tracks. Restrictor plates are thin squares of aluminum with four holes. They reduce airflow from the carburetor into the engine, resulting in less horsepower and speed. Qualifying speeds at Talladega dropped by more than ten miles an hour. But not everyone thinks the races there are safer. Drivers at restrictor plate tracks often grumble that the packs of cars are too close. Often, "The Big One," a smoky, chaotic wreck, will eliminate half the field from contention. For that reason, many of the drivers think that restrictor plates make the races more dangerous.

True story: The Nascar Winston Cup driver Kenny Schrader is driving his racecar, screaming around the track at 180 miles an hour. He is also on his radio with his crew.

Schrader looks ahead and sees the spinning cars, shrapnel, and awful smoke screen that mean a wreck. "Gotta go," he tells the crew. "I'm about to get real busy."

It has been repeated so often that it is practically legend by now, and Schrader no longer remembers which race that was. The fact is, he said, "You get real busy a lot of times."

The question is, busy doing what? You're speeding along with fingertip control of a 3,500-pound racecar, and suddenly you see trouble ahead. Or worse—you're cruising along, and suddenly somebody ticks you in the back, or you just go too deep into a turn and the car lifts. You're no longer driving a racecar; you're part of a physics experiment.

What, exactly, can you do?

The most common trouble a racecar gets into is a spin, in which the rear of the car starts to come counterclockwise around the front. The first thing a driver will do in that situation is release the throttle—lift—and hope the car settles down. If the car is sliding sideways, the driver might accelerate to try to get some rear-wheel grip.

The next response is a light turn to the right.

"If I can't gather it up at that point," said the driver Ricky Rudd, "it's time to lock it down"—that is, hit the brakes and hope for the best.

"After your fate is set, and you know you're going to be in a wreck, I shove my head in the seat—that seems to minimize the whipping effect," he said, and other drivers agreed. Jeff Burton added: "Anything you can do to minimize motion during a wreck is good. . . . When the car is definitely backing toward the wall, you'll get hard into the gas," meaning the forward motion of the tires will help slow the backward motion of the car.

Rudd tried to explain. "Even if you're going backward, you're still driving the car." And it's not just your own safety that's at stake—there's also the safety of forty-two other cars barreling toward your out-of-control car at 180 miles per hour.

As a driver approaching trouble, "you usually get one shot to minimize a wreck," Rudd said. "You got to get a read on the wreck, and you get one chance." You're moving so quickly that a couple of sudden steering corrections are likely to throw your own car out of control.

The driver Steve Park said that avoiding a wreck was mostly luck anyway. "Eighty percent luck, twenty percent driver," he said of avoiding a crash. His one rule? "You go where the accident started, because they never end up where they start," he said.

Reading that wreck, in a way, is a driver's most vital skill, and his hardest earned: it comes only through experience.

"Lap after lap it's the same thing, and all of a sudden you see something different," Tony Stewart said, describing the sport from behind the wheel. You do what you can, but often enough, Stewart said, it just ends up out of control, with a long, empty ride toward a wall.

"That's a long way to slide," he said. "And you're like, 'Well, when's it going to hit?'"

Stewart said that maybe the long-retired Richard Petty had the best idea. When asked why he drove such a high line around most tracks, Petty had a stock response: then he didn't have to go so far to hit the wall.

Race teams try to squeeze every precious bit of speed from a car while following a long list of precise rules. Some details are open to interpretation—like the way the tires are tilted on a car to handle the high banking at many racetracks.

Each car in a Nascar race must go through a rigorous inspection. Sheet-metal "templates" are used to measure the cars to ensure that no one has even the tiniest advantage. Winning cars are inspected after a race to determine that they won fairly.

Nascar's founder, William France (known as Big Bill), believed that the series would lose popularity if one car, or cars made by a particular manufacturer, dominated. The top stock cars are American-made. Ford, Chevrolet, and Dodge compete hard for victories and prize money from week to week. So if one manufacturer lags behind the others, the rules are tweaked to even the odds.

Not surprisingly, these rule changes often anger those with the fastest cars, who feel they are being denied an advantage—especially when the changes are made after the start of a season. But Nascar wants tight competition. Ideally, most of the cars in a race should stand a chance to win. In fact, in any single season, only fifteen to twenty different drivers will win a race.

Inspection: Sheet-metal "templates" are used to measure the cars to ensure no one has even the smallest advantage.

Although stock cars are no longer truly "stock" cars, there are still stock parts on them. For example, General Motors provides the hood of the car, the roof, and the rear deck lid—what would normally be a trunk lid—to its racing teams so all the Chevrolets in the races look the same. Actually, all forty-three cars in the race look pretty much the same. It is what is inside the car that makes the difference.

The top racing teams have dozens of employees who build

cars from scratch. They spend millions of dollars to find the technology and do the testing to develop winning cars. The length of races and even the length of the tracks vary greatly. A driver may appear to be driving the same car every week, but most teams build different cars for the different tracks—superspeedways, shorter ovals, flatter tracks, and road courses. The Nextel Cup series has two races on road courses—racetracks that are not ovals but have many turns, left and right, within one lap. These races, at tracks in Sonoma, California, and Watkins Glen, New York, are popular among drivers who relish the extra challenge.

In 1990, Hendrick Motorsports, which later added Jeff Gordon as a driver, was the first team to create its own engineering department, which developed the chassis, or the steel frame, of its racecars. Building a car is a very detailed process. Before Hendrick Motorsports finishes a chassis, it puts it through a rigorous inspection. The chassis must be durable enough to finish a punishing race. Many races are lost simply because of one flawed part in a racecar that went undetected until it was too late.

The company has nearly a hundred employees who work on race engines alone. They build more than seven hundred engines a year for Hendrick's race teams, as well as

Crews spend hundreds of hours building, testing, and maintaining their racecars' engines.

for other teams who lease engines from the company. A race engine is not expected to last for years and years like the engine in a passenger car does, but it must generate plenty of horsepower and last for an entire race, which is no small feat. A driver may be leading the pack in a fast car only to slow down suddenly because his engine malfunctioned.

A small flaw, undetected, can have disastrous results.

An engine is taken apart after it runs at the racetrack. The parts are examined and tested. Pistons, valves, and springs are replaced. Other parts are reused, but Hendrick estimates that an engine will be used fifteen or twenty times at most before it is retired.

Drivers often mention "dyno" machines when they talk about a successful car. These are engine dynamometers—stationary machines in the shop on which engines can be mounted, connected to fuel lines, and run under simulated race conditions.

The engine's performance is measured to determine if it meets standards and is high enough to put in a racecar.

A "spintron" can even mimic the conditions of a particular track to see how the engine will respond.

There are also chassis dynamometers, which measure the chassis' response to simulated racing conditions, and cars are also placed in wind tunnels, where large fans pump wind over the body of a car to see how efficiently it slips through the resistance.

A race engine weighs more than five hundred pounds and costs between $45,000 and $60,000 to build. Typically, teams take three engines to a race: one each for the two cars they haul to the track, and a spare just in case something happens to the other two.

Hundreds of hours are spent on research before a car is built, and when it is finished the driver has to test it. Some drivers don't enjoy this. Dale Earnhardt Jr., for one, finds test sessions extremely boring. But what the drivers discover during a test session is important. They learn how the cars will handle the characteristics of the racetracks. They can tell their crew chiefs how the cars feel at top speeds so the chiefs can make adjustments.

The most important relationship on a race team may be the one between the driver and crew chief. Tony Stewart is a fierce competitor and smooth driver who seems to know just how hard he can push his car. But Stewart has often said he is no mechanic.

Hendrick Motorsports has almost one hundred employees who only work on racecar engines.

His crew chief, Greg Zipadelli, is not just knowledgeable about the workings of a racecar; he knows how to process Stewart's comments to make the needed adjustments to the car. Stewart is known to be temperamental—sometimes curt with reporters, sometimes sullen after losing a race he thought he should have won. But Zipadelli seems to be able to calmly process Stewart's complaints into solutions that help him drive faster.

"He's the leader," Stewart says of his crew chief. "He's always had to baby-sit me a lot, which has taken me out of the position to make decisions. We're just a good combination. It's kind of like a marriage."

Practice sessions take place before races, giving teams a chance to fine-tune their cars. Any one of dozens of adjustments can be made between practice runs to get the cars to handle better, especially on the corners.

One of the most common complaints from drivers is that a car is "loose" or "tight." A tight car is hard to steer; a loose car can fishtail around a curve. The crew can adjust springs that change the pressure on the tires to fix the problem.

The garages are busy during practice sessions. Quite often a driver will take a car out for a few laps, not like what he feels, and bring it back to the garage, where the crew will tinker with it as the driver, still in his seat, tells his crew chief what he is feeling.

There is the clatter of tools and an occasional roar of a revved engine. Practice time is limited, so every minute counts. A qualifying session is held one or two days before the race, setting the starting positions.

Then comes the race.

A car that belonged to Junior Johnson, an early stock-car legend, on view at the Appalachian Cultural Museum in Boone, North Carolina.

Darrell Waltrip often likes to holler, "Boogity, boogity, boogity!" as the cars reach high speed. Fans wave signs. Everybody wants the cars to go even faster. The sheer speed of the cars is thrilling.

Because the top cars are so evenly matched, a race is often determined by people who spend much of the race hunched near the wall next to the pits—the pit crew. Not that long ago, most pit crews were made up of friends and relatives of the drivers. They wore T-shirts and blue jeans and serviced the car with care, but not at great speed. As stock car racing became more competitive, speed in the pits became essential. A speedy pit crew can win a race. There are many caution periods during a typical Nextel Cup race. The cars must slow down behind a pace car as the track is cleaned up. Most teams use this time to make a pit stop.

Drivers in the lead positions will often make pit stops at the same time. It is a hectic and chaotic time on pit road, but if a car's crew can turn a particularly fast pit stop, the car can jump from, say, fifth place to first place. It is much harder to pass cars on the track.

Practice time is limited, so every minute counts.

Quick stop: A good Nascar pit crew can change a pair of tires and top up the gas tank in less than fifteen seconds.

What goes on in the pits when the racers duck in for fuel and tires is as much a part of the show for stock car racing fans as the dozen cars drafting nose to tail at two hundred miles per hour around the banking. A good Nascar pit crew can change a pair of tires and top up the gas tank in fewer than twelve seconds.

At the big tracks, such as the 2.5-mile Pocono International Raceway in Mount Pocono, Pennsylvania, it's possible to drive faster in a tight bunch of cars than alone. The strategy is to stay in touch with the lead pack until the last few laps and then attempt to break away.

Buddy Parrott, a pit crew manager, summed it up twenty years ago in a statement that's as true today as it was then: "If you spend an extra five seconds in the pits and lose the draft, you can just about write yourself off."

Although it sometimes looks as if the crews are simply scrambling around a car, there is choreography to what they do, as with a dance routine. First, the driver must park the car inside the yellow square that is designated as the team's pit. Then the crew, dressed in fire suits like the drivers, gets to work.

Dale Earnhardt Jr.'s pit crew doing what it does best.

Nascar allows seven crew members over the wall during a pit stop; sometimes it will allow an eighth member to clean the windshield. During a routine stop, the crew clambers first to the right-side wheels.

A jackman places a hydraulic jack under the outside of the car to lift it high enough to change the tires. Two tire changers—one front, one back—use noisy drills to loosen five lug nuts and remove the used tires.

Tire carriers hand the tire changers two new tires. The tire changers use the wrenches to attach the tires to the car with five lug nuts. The car is lowered on the jack, and the group repeats the process on the two left tires.

In the meantime, two crew members fill the fuel cell. A gasman empties two tall red twelve-gallon cans of gasoline into the car. A catch-can man collects the fuel that spills out. He gives the driver a wave, and the car peels away.

Here is the most amazing part: a routine four-tire pit stop takes about fifteen seconds. Teams sometimes push their luck and change only two tires, or take only fuel, so they can gain position.

Things in the pit do not always go well. A lug nut may not be attached. The jack may break. A driver can overshoot his pit. A car may need a major adjustment. The driver can stall the car while trying to speed away.

To ensure safety and prevent accidents, there is a speed limit on pit road, and drivers who go too fast or do not make a clean pit stop are penalized.

So, when Tony Stewart wins a race, it is not just because he has driven the fastest: his team has provided him with a competitive car, made the necessary adjustments, and given him lots of support during the race.

But even the most determined group efforts do not guarantee

success. Sometimes the parts in an engine disintegrate, causing the car to suddenly lose speed and chug slowly around the track, trailing large clouds of gray-white smoke.

> *The first sign of disaster can be a puff of smoke out of the tailpipe after a piston goes in the engine. Then the car seemingly starts going backward, 200 miles an hour to 180, then to 160. It is finally dragged behind the pit road wall, another victim of Nascar's fastest track.*
>
> *No track is tougher on engines than Atlanta Motor Speedway, where cars can go into the first turn at 205 to 208 miles per hour and where drivers can be on the throttle for more than three hours. The race here is also one of the longest events on the circuit.*
>
> *"You're running almost wide open the whole time around here; you're running a lot of reps, so it is really hard on the internals of the engine," said Matt Borland, the crew chief for the driver Ryan Newman, in the 2005 race at Atlanta.*
>
> *The track is notoriously tough on engines. Nine engines were blown during a race in 2003. Five engines broke in a 2004 race.*
>
> *"But you can't think about engine trouble," said Borland. "You have to just go."*

Or a car might run over a sharp piece of debris with its thick no-tread tires, causing a blowout that could lead to a wreck. A rough patch of track at Pocono Raceway in Pennsylvania led to the blowouts of more than twenty left-side front tires at one race in 2005.

"Tire problems happen because we abuse them," Dale Jarrett, a veteran driver, told me in a 2005 interview. "We do things to them that they weren't built to do."

After the race, Nascar officials rigorously check the winning car to see if the crew followed every rule and specification to win fairly. Disqualifications are rare, but that doesn't mean that teams have not tried to bend the rules over the years. Racing historians say that cheating used to be a sport unto itself in stock car racing.

My favorite story involved Darrell Waltrip's car in the 1980s. Gary Nelson, Waltrip's crew chief, was said to fill the steel roll cage of his car with several pounds of lead buckshot so it would be heavy enough to meet race requirements. But after the race started, Waltrip would pull a lever and the buckshot would pour onto the track. The car would weigh much less than the other cars and as a result would go a lot faster. Waltrip would yell over his radio the words, "Bombs away!" to let Nelson know that the buckshot was gone.

Even the most determined efforts can't stop some mishaps—like blowouts.

Nelson later became a Nascar official, and he has never admitted to using buckshot. Whether it's true, or just another racing legend, you certainly don't hear too many stories like that now. Too much money is on the line to risk disqualification.

FOUR
History
"We're Getting More Roots"

The first turn at Dover International Speedway is as good a point as any for watching a stock car race. Tall grandstands almost completely ring the one-mile track in central Delaware, which is called the "Monster Mile" because it is so demanding on the drivers. With its high bank, the racetrack chews away tires and punishes the cars during long races. When drivers climb out of their cars after races at the Monster Mile, their fire suits are often soaked through with sweat.

Since 1971, the Monster Mile has played host to two races yearly in Nascar's top series. Until 1997, the races at Dover were five hundred miles, or five hundred laps. Because the track was smaller, cars went slower, and the races usually took four hours to complete.

I didn't know that when I settled into my press-box seat near turn one at Dover on June 3, 1990. I was excited about seeing my first Nascar race. I'd just returned from covering my first Indianapolis 500 when I was asked to report on the Dover race.

Dover was nothing like Indianapolis, where thirty-three sleek, aerodynamic open-wheel racecars run on a two-and-a-half-mile oval. There are forty-three stock cars, slower and heavier than Indy cars, in a Nascar race.

Bill Elliott led the pack to the starting line. Mark Martin started second in a car that was the same reddish color as a Folgers coffee can, because he was sponsored by the company. The cars tilted as they moved around the high banks, sweeping around the first two turns and then flattening out on the backstretch, buzzing like hornets.

They pitched again on an alarming angle as they went around the third and fourth turns before they crossed the start-finish line and did it all over again. From time to time, cars thumped into each other—it seemed to be an accomplishment just to finish the race in one piece.

Derrike Cope won the race in just under four hours. I felt as exhausted as Cope must have been, just from watching the pack of cars make one lap after another, hundreds of times, as what had begun as a bright afternoon began to turn to dusk. A week earlier, Arie Luyendyk had won the Indy 500 in less than three hours. Even though Luyendyk had won a more famous race, Cope looked a lot more tired.

I learned that day how different stock car racing can be from Indy car racing. Stock car racing is more about endurance than exotic speed. Stock cars look more like the cars that ordinary people drive. Stock car drivers are almost all Americans, and all cars carry the names of American auto factories.

Stock car races have been run since Americans were able to buy cars in the early 1900s. But until 1947, when William H. G. France called a meeting in Daytona Beach, stock car racing was not well organized.

Monster Mile: Dover International Speedway chews tires and punishes engines.

Before that, in the very early days, stock car drivers raced on the weekends and used those same hot rods during the week to run "moonshine," or homemade liquor, past cars driven by federal and local agents.

During Prohibition, which ran from 1919 until 1933 in the United States, liquor was illegal. There was still a demand for it, though, and some people who lived in rural areas made and sold illegal "moonshine" whiskey. After Prohibition, many continued "moonshining," making the whiskey without following government regulations. They needed deliverymen to get the moonshine to buyers without paying taxes, and these deliverymen—often called "bootleggers"—used souped-up cars to outrun the police.

In their spare time, the bootleggers would meet and stage races to see who had the fastest car. Soon, more and more people who weren't involved in bootlegging began to participate and came to watch the races. Because liquor was still illegal in some municipalities after Prohibition, there were still bootleggers, hot rods, and weekend races into the 1940s.

A moonshine still in Tennessee.

Police capture a moonshine smuggler, known as a bootlegger, during the Prohibition era.

Stock car racing's origins in bootlegging left a tradition of swashbuckling legends. One story is about a Carolinian in the late 1940s who ran moonshine to the city in his car on Friday night, raced on the weekend, and on Monday morning loaded up with sugar and headed back to the stills in the hills. One Sunday, while leading a race, he was puzzled by an unfamiliar signal from his pit crew. Then he reasoned it out: some government agents were waiting to arrest him. So he took the checkered flag, swept through turns one and two on what looked like a victory lap, then plowed through the fence at turn three onto a backwoods road—and he was home free.

Big Bill France, who stood six foot five, was not involved in bootlegging, but he liked to race cars. In the 1930s he moved to Daytona Beach and opened a gas station. Shortly afterward he started racing on a famous track in town that included local roads and a stretch of hard-packed sand on the beach itself. As a business owner, he knew that it would help the local economy if he could keep people coming to town all year round, not just during the winter months, when northerners came to Daytona Beach on vacation.

Big Bill France
established the Nascar
blueprint in 1947.

William H. G. France, known as "Big Bill," founded Nascar in 1948 and was its first president. Since then, the Frances have become known as stock car racing's "royal family." His son, William C. France, took over his position as head of Nascar in 1972, and his grandson, Brian, became Nascar's chairman of the board and chief executive officer in 2003.

Big Bill France also founded International Speedway Corp., which owns Daytona International Speedway, Talladega Superspeedway, and several other tracks used in Nascar races.

The France family is often criticized for holding too much control over stock car racing. As the heads of Nascar, they have determined which tracks will host races, set and changed the rules, and, through those rules, affected who was allowed to participate in races.

Big Bill France, who died in 1992, was often portrayed as a willful, imperious man who was all but the emperor of Nascar, but he won many admirers who saw him as a visionary.

What is indisputable is the Frances' record of success, which has made a great deal of money for many Nascar promoters and teams. It seems likely that the royal family of Nascar will continue to reign for many years to come.

In December 1947, Big Bill France called a meeting at the Streamline Hotel in Daytona Beach. He sat at the head of the table, and about two dozen racing promoters, drivers, and mechanics sat around it. They decided to form an organization for stock car racing that included standards for the cars and drivers and rules for every race. Until then, races had been haphazard and slapdash. France felt that an organization would establish uniformity, and the races, in turn, could be promoted by one organization to draw even more fans. The elite division would be called "Strictly Stock" because the racecars would come from an automobile showroom—or be built from parts that were in stock.

The first race organized by the new group was run on February 15, 1948. Red Byron won the race, which was such a success that the National Association for Stock Car Auto Racing, or Nascar, was incorporated six days later. The new organization held races in several states, with a standard set of rules—and officials who made sure those rules were followed. Jim Roper was listed as the winner of the first race in Charlotte, North Carolina, on June 19, 1949, but only after a driver named Glenn Dunnaway, who had come in first, was disqualified for using illegal suspension parts in his car, which he also used to run moonshine. The first full season included eight races. Byron won two of them and the championship.

Even in the early days, most drivers raced in cars owned by others. Pit crews were made up of mostly friends and relatives who knew something about cars. Many of the drivers were more like

Cars built from extra stock parts race on Daytona Beach's hard-packed sand in the 1940s.

swashbucklers than athletes; men like Robert "Red" Byron raced for the thrill and challenge. They certainly did not drive for the money: Byron, whose car was owned by Raymond Parks, made only $10,100 in fifteen career starts. Like most of the competition, he grew up in the South and began racing as a teenager. According to racing lore, Byron was a tail-gunner on a B-24 bomber during World War II. His plane was shot down, and doctors had to rebuild his left leg. It was thought that Byron would never walk again, but he returned to racecars. He had to put his left leg in a stirrup that was bolted to the clutch.

Most but not all of the races were held in the Southeast, with a few held that season at tracks outside Philadelphia, Buffalo, and Pittsburgh. Not everyone had enough money to drive in every race, but the races were competitive and popular.

Nineteen races were scheduled for the 1950 season. France changed the name of the top series from "Strictly Stock" to "Grand

Early racing was often dangerous. Here, a driver is thrown clear of his car as it rolls over during a race.

National," and that year the drivers, who were used to competing on short or dirt tracks, competed for the first time on a paved "superspeedway." The 1.3-mile paved track was built near Darlington, South Carolina, in the northeastern corner of the state. Harold Brasington, a local businessman, wanted to convert a field used to grow cotton and peanuts into another Indianapolis Motor Speedway. But he had to make some concessions to the landowner, who had a favorite fishing hole at one end of the property. Brasington had to change the shape of his racetrack to be more egg- than oval-shaped so that the pond would not be disturbed.

The first Southern 500 was held there on September 4, 1950. Brasington expected a crowd of 10,000, but more than 25,000 showed up. Seventy-five drivers started the race, which took six hours. The winner, Johnny Mantz, averaged 75.251 miles an hour..

The Darlington track gave the Grand National series a Labor Day showpiece. The series grew to forty-one races in 1951, forty-five races in 1955, and then leapt to fifty-six races in 1956. Lee Petty, a driver from Level Cross, North Carolina, won three championships in the 1950s. Driving a white Oldsmobile, Petty also won the first Daytona 500 in February 1959, held on a new speedway that Big Bill France had built. France had decided that the old racetrack in Daytona Beach was obsolete, so he built a two-and-a-half-mile superspeedway outside town.

Nascar was becoming more and more popular at home; all it lacked was a superstar whose appeal could stretch beyond the southeastern United States.

In 1965, the writer Tom Wolfe showed up at a race at

The Nascar hierarchy in 1972: Big Bill and his son, William C. France.

When Daytona International Speedway was completed in February 1958, it was America's fastest speedway. Until then, sports car racers usually competed on flat or slightly banked, twisting courses. Daytona's speedway combined a 1.3-mile flat and curving course with 2.5 miles of high-speed, 31-degree banked asphalt.

In a five-hundred-mile stock car race that opened the track to big-time competition, the average speed of the winner was better than 135 miles an hour. And the finish of the race was so close that the final result was not recorded until after a week of study of photographs and moving pictures, which separated Lee Petty, the North Carolina star in an Oldsmobile, and Johnny Beauchamp of Iowa in a Thunderbird.

Today cars can travel faster than two hundred miles an hour at high-banked tracks such as Daytona and Talladega.

The Firecracker 250 in 1960, when the Daytona race track was brand new.

North Wilkesboro, North Carolina, to write a magazine article about Junior Johnson. Tom Wolfe had been born in the South, but he lived in New York; he wrote for the *New York*

Tom Wolfe

Herald Tribune and national magazines that had a wide readership. Johnson was a good driver, but not the best. What made him such an interesting story to Wolfe was that Johnson had been a bootlegger who was good at sneaking cars loaded with jars of moonshine past police. But Johnson had been caught at his father's still in the woods, so he had served time in prison. Junior Johnson was handsome and gregarious. His talent as a driver, not to mention his scrapes with the law, made him popular with teenage girls, who swarmed around him. He was the kind of guy a mother most definitely did not want her daughter dating, much less bringing home.

Wolfe was captivated by the scene at the race. The crowd—only 17,000, very small by today's standards—fought a massive traffic jam to watch Johnson and others race. Wolfe was also amazed at the spectacle of a race itself.

Wolfe spent a lot of time with Johnson and wrote in depth about Johnson's appeal to race fans in North Carolina, his home state. Johnson was adored for his ability to drive a car in a sport that, at the time, not many people outside the Southeast knew much about.

Probably because of Johnson's background, Nascar does not include the article about him in its list of famous moments. But Tom Wolfe's article may have nudged the sport into the American mainstream. Johnson won fifty races in his career, which ended in 1966, the year after the article appeared. The Grand National series would come to be dominated by another popular driver from Level Cross, North Carolina: Richard Petty, Lee's son—a man any mother would love.

Richard Petty joined the Grand National series in 1958. He won 200 races and seven championships in his thirty-five-year career, earning his nickname of "the King." David Pearson, who

Junior Johnson (center) was immortalized in an article by Tom Wolfe.

is next on the all-time list, won only 105. Petty won twenty-seven races in the 1967 season, including an astounding ten in a row. No other driver won more than six races that season. Even when Petty had an off year, he still won a lot: he finished third in the 1968 point standings, but he won sixteen races.

Petty was much more than a talented driver. He walked around the garage with a regal air—usually wearing a cowboy hat with a feather, wraparound sunglasses, a Western shirt, and blue jeans. But he had a reputation for being approachable and unfailingly friendly. Anyone who wanted his autograph got a big, looping signature, plus a wide smile and a brief conversation. All those years of racing had made him hard of hearing, but Petty always craned his neck closer to a fan in an attempt to catch every word.

After Petty won his third championship in 1971, he signed a sponsorship contract with STP, a company that makes gasoline and oil additives. Until then, most Grand National cars had been sponsored by local companies, or sponsored by big national firms for only a few races.

STP painted its big red logo across the hood of Petty's famous blue Chrysler with the number 43 on the roof and sides. Petty won eight races and his fourth championship in 1972, so the STP logo was seen during all of the races that were televised. Other corporations noticed.

Richard Petty became known as "the King."

Nascar was changing, and in a big way. Big Bill France oversaw the construction of a superspeedway that was even bigger and faster than Daytona. Alabama International Speedway, near the town of Talladega, opened in September 1969.

The track, which eventually came to be known as Talladega Superspeedway, was bigger than Daytona, with higher banking in the corners and a much longer backstretch in which drivers could travel at incredibly high speeds for the time—as much as 135 miles per hour.

Reason to smile: Petty won eight races and his fourth championship in 1972.

Big Bill France retired in 1972 and passed the Nascar presidency on to his son, also named Bill. But before Big Bill France left his post, he struck a sponsorship deal with the R. J. Reynolds Tobacco Company that would dramatically alter the sport.

R. J. Reynolds gave money to Nascar in exchange for being able to advertise its products at the Nascar racetracks. In 1971, the Grand National series became known as the Winston Cup series after one of the company's cigarette brands.

Those sponsorship dollars gave Big Bill France a chance to streamline what had become an unwieldy series. There were forty-eight races in the 1970 Grand National series, including some run on dirt tracks or small tracks. In order to make enough money for the teams to keep running, Nascar needed to hold frequent races so they could sell a lot of tickets. The racing schedule was cluttered, with races sometimes only days apart. That meant that even the stars were not able to run in every race, which didn't sit well with France. He wanted to build a racing league at only the best facilities around the sport's top performers.

By 1972, the schedule had been pared to thirty-one races. There were events in California, Michigan, Texas, and New Jersey, but the bulk of the races were still in the Southeast. The top six drivers in the 1972 point standings drove in every race.

Known as a "superspeedway," Talladega has high banks that allow speeds in excess of 200 mph.

Petty dominated the races in the 1970s, winning championships in 1974, 1975, and 1979. Pearson, Bobby Allison, and Cale Yarborough were worthy competitors, but it seemed as if it was Petty and then everyone else. The sport needed another star.

Many drivers in those days earned just enough to cover their expenses. Before a race in 1990, I talked to one driver who had been racing since the 1970s, J. D. McDuffie, a cigar-chomping native of North Carolina. He owned and managed his race team, built engines, drove the car, and answered the shop telephone. McDuffie's blue and yellow Pontiac, number 70, was unadorned by the name of a major corporate sponsor. When he was killed on August 11, 1991, during a race at Watkins Glen, New York, McDuffie was fifty-two years old and had driven in 653 Grand National and Winston Cup races from 1963 to 1991 without winning a single one. He drove because racing was his life. If he did not race, he told me, he did not eat.

"J.D. loves racing, loves people, loves travel," Richard Petty told me in 1990. "As long as he makes a living out of it, what else is there? He has had to make what he gets out of the purses pay the bills. The cost of everything has gone up so much. It's getting so expensive that you can't live without the sponsors. If you won half the races, maybe you could."

Dale Earnhardt's father, Ralph, also raced because he loved it. Ralph Earnhardt, driving car number 8,

J. D. McDuffie, shown here in 1974, raced without sponsorship.

which his grandson would make famous someday, was talented, but he preferred to race on tracks near his home. He died of heart failure in 1973 while working on his car. He was just forty-five years old. Dale Earnhardt was deeply saddened, but he also was motivated to race as hard as his father had. Sometimes Dale Earnhardt made just enough money to pay for new parts for his cars. But Earnhardt won the Winston Cup championship in 1980 and, after he joined Richard Childress's team, won two more by 1987.

Earnhardt was joined in the series by new, young drivers. The gregarious Darrell Waltrip, from Owensboro, Kentucky, won eighty-four races in his career, including championships in 1981, 1982, and 1985. Bill Elliott, a quiet, red-haired Georgia native who was nicknamed "Awesome Bill from Dawsonville," won the 1988 championship. Rusty Wallace, a wisecracking redhead from St. Louis, won the championship in 1989. Petty retired in 1992, but new stars packed the series.

There was room for one more talented driver who would give the Winston Cup series a push into the next century. Petty's last race was at Atlanta Motor Speedway on November 15, 1992, and not many people noticed the twenty-one-year-old driver who finished thirty-first in his first Winston Cup race.

That driver, Jeff Gordon, had grown up in California and moved with his family when he

Bill Elliot: "Awesome Bill from Dawsonville."

was a teenager to Pittsboro, Indiana, fourteen miles from Indianapolis, so he could pursue a career as an Indy car driver. But in stock cars he had more opportunities to race, and there he found a smoother path to success.

By 1991 Gordon was driving in the Busch series, Nascar's second-level racing circuit, and by 1993 he was driving full-time on the Winston Cup series for Rick Hendrick. Two years later, he won the first of four Winston Cup championships in a seven-year span in his number 24 Chevrolet.

In 1994, Gordon also won the first Nascar race at the Indianapolis Motor Speedway; the hallowed track that is the capital of Indy car racing. The Brickyard 400 quickly became Nascar's second-biggest race, behind only Daytona.

Jeff Gordon's crew services his famous number 24 Chevrolet.

As two Indy car factions battled throughout the late 1990s, pushing Nascar into national prominence, the Brickyard 400, packing the great gray grandstands, became more popular than the Indianapolis 500.

"Every time I drive into this facility, I'm in awe of it, and I've driven it a thousand times," Gordon said before the 2003 Brickyard 400.

Gordon was everything Earnhardt was not, most notably clean-cut and well spoken. He married a woman named Brooke Sealy, who had been one of the beauty queens known as "Miss Winston" in the series, and the handsome couple was sort of like the prom king and queen of stock cars. Perhaps even more important, Gordon did not speak with a southern accent. Those who liked Earnhardt tended not to like Gordon. To them, he was a goody two-shoes.

A rivalry was born, though the two drivers respected each other. In 1995, Earnhardt grumbled that Gordon was so young that he would have to drink milk instead of champagne at the season-ending banquet. Gordon won the title and toasted Earnhardt at the banquet with a glass of milk. Earnhardt smiled. He won the last of his seven Winston Cup championships in 1994, but Gordon always seemed to make him drive a little faster.

Dale Earnhardt Jr. made his debut as a full-time driver on the Winston Cup series in 1999. Dale Jr. was brash and fast, and years later, after his father was killed, Dale Jr. replaced him as Gordon's rival. But Earnhardt was not

Gordon's only competition. Dale Jr. was followed into the series by a group of drivers called the Young Guns.

Earnhardt was a North Carolinian, but most of the other Young Guns were not from the South. Kevin Harvick, Dale Sr.'s successor, grew up in Bakersfield, California. Matt Kenseth was from Cambridge, Wisconsin. Jimmie Johnson, Gordon's teammate, was from El Cajon, California, and Kurt Busch was from Las Vegas.

Nascar had become the place to be, and drivers from all over the country were migrating to it. The schedule was altered to appeal to fans nationwide. Nascar announced in 2003 that the Southern 500, the Labor Day tradition at Darlington, would be moved to another date to make room for a race near Los Angeles.

But there would be one more change, an even bigger change, that would signal the start of yet another era in stock car racing.

On June 19, 2003, at a television studio in a building in Times Square in New York, with laser lights slicing through the darkness, Nascar officials announced that they had landed a new sponsorship deal with Nextel, a telecommunications corporation.

The deal was for ten years and was worth $700 million. With Nextel, there were no restrictions on advertising, as there had been when R. J. Reynolds was its sponsor. As a tobacco manufacturer, R. J. Reynolds was prohibited from advertising its products on television and radio (ironically, advertising was one of the reasons the company had decided to sponsor Nascar racing in the first place). But the advertising ban affected Nascar, because R. J. Reynolds could not air commercials for one of its most popular cigarette brands—Winston.

Now Nascar had a cutting-edge sponsor who could help sell stock car racing to yet another generation of young fans. Before the news conference started, Bill France Jr. sat in a quiet room next to the television studio and softly told me, "We're not moving away from our roots. We're getting more roots."

Bill France Jr. was just a boy when his father organized the series that would one day be named after a company that made cellular phones. The days of racing on the sands of Daytona Beach seemed very, very far in the past.

Sponsor signs like this one at the Martinsville Speedway in West Virginia are everywhere at Nascar tracks.

FIVE

The Fans
"We've Made It to the Big Time"

A tall set of bleachers in the infield at Pocono Raceway does not provide a very good vantage point to watch a Nextel Cup race, but it is a popular place with fans. The bleachers perch next to an access road that leads from the garages to the big, triangle-shaped racetrack. A chainlink fence separates the bleachers from the road. A couple of holes have been cut into the fence, and wooden planks have been set at the bottom of each hole, about four feet off the ground, making the holes look a little like ticket booths.

This is "Autograph Alley." Usually, drivers whiz to and from their garages, eyes fixed ahead. But sometimes they walk from the track to the garage and stop by here to meet with fans.

It's a good place to see why Nascar has become so popular. When a driver ambles past, fans who have gathered in the bleachers scamper down to the holes in the fence to push through a piece of paper or a model car to be signed. It seems as if every driver knows to keep a felt-tip marker in the pants of his driving suit for just such a moment. Even the most famous ones will pause to sign autographs or quickly pose for snapshots.

At the Daytona International Speedway a couple of years ago, Dale Jarrett, a veteran driver, had just finished an interview with reporters in the media center. As he strolled back to the garage, a fan asked him to stop and smile. Jarrett did. The fan snapped a photo and Jarrett was soon on his way. He had posed for many photos like that in his long career. But to the fan it was a special moment. He exclaimed to a friend, "I've waited three years to get that photo!"

Nascar's reputation is built on its accessibility. Fans have access to the stars that is unheard of in most other sports. Some fans receive passes to roam the garages and the area behind the pits before practices and races. Imagine being able to sit in the dugout during a major league baseball game, or to visit the locker room before a football game to chat with the starting quarterback.

Two hours before a race at the New Hampshire International Speedway in September 2005, hundreds of fans gathered in the area between the garages and the big tractor-trailers. They hoped to catch a glimpse of a driver, and they were not disappointed. Driver after driver had to walk through the crowds to get from his team's trailer to his car, which was parked on the track.

The number of Nascar fans has skyrocketed since 2001, and

Tony Stewart signs autographs for fans at a soap-box race sponsored by Home Depot.

increased television exposure has played a huge role. Every Nextel Cup race is on network television now, and millions tune in. But there was a time when only a few stock car races were on television.

The 2001 Daytona 500, the race in which Dale Earnhardt was killed, was the first race carried by the Fox network as part of an eight-year contract. NBC signed a six-year contract to carry the second half of the schedule beginning in July 2001.

Fox aired some races on FX, its cable network partner, and NBC aired some on TNT, its cable partner. Every race is available to viewers with cable television.

Prior to 1998, only the big races were televised. Fans sometimes had to go to movie theaters to see live broadcasts of races. CBS didn't air the first live flag-to-flag coverage of the Daytona 500, the premier stock car race, until 1979. ABC had shown previous Daytona 500s but would only join the race about halfway through. Nascar had a lot of catching up to do with other sports, and it did so quickly.

On network or cable, from above or on the ground, every Nascar race is televised.

In the last decade or so, as stock car racing's popularity has climbed, drivers have become as visible on television as any entertainment personality. Dale Earnhardt Jr. has done dozens of television commercials for different products. And in 2003, Jeff Gordon hosted *Saturday Night Live*.

Nascar has tried to retain its appeal as a sport in which its stars can be seen in person by the fans. Before almost every race, the drivers are introduced on a stage. Or they hop into trucks and are driven around the track, waving like heroes in a parade.

As in a soap opera, there are good guys and bad guys—and sometimes drivers can be both. Jeff Gordon, clean-cut, personable, and successful, would seem to be a good guy. But the fans of Dale Earnhardt Jr. don't seem to think so. Earnhardt Sr. had the reputation among his fans as a rebel, a driver who would knock anyone out of the way, but he could not intimidate Gordon.

Now, when Dale Jr. or Gordon takes the lead late in a race, there is simultaneous cheering and booing. The two drivers are competitors, but their fans like to think of them more as enemies.

A spicy feud between stock car drivers has a much shorter shelf life inside a racetrack than outside. Two drivers involved in a wreck usually grumble, sometimes curse, then put their broken cars into the hauler to hustle to another race.

"You've got to realize we're all a part of a traveling circus thirty-eight weeks a year," Chad Knaus, the crew chief for Jimmie Johnson, said. "If you sit there and hold a grudge over somebody else's head, you're only going to hurt yourself."

After an accident during a race in May 2005, Johnson appeared to be sitting in a stewpot of simmering disagreement with Tony Stewart.

But when he was interviewed a week later, Stewart said the accident might as well have happened ten years before. "We had an accident," Stewart said. "Accidents happen. It's over. It's done with. In fact, here it is Friday, and it's kind of annoying talking about something that happened last Saturday."

Sometimes perceptions change. Tony Stewart was a talented Indy driver who joined Nascar in 1998. He won a championship in 2002, but for several years he was thought to be a hothead.

After the 2004 season, Stewart had a meeting with his team. His crew told him that he needed to control his temper. His surly behavior, which once included taking a punch at a newspaper photographer, was distracting the team from doing its job well.

Stewart realized they were right. He tried to become friendlier to his team and more engaging with the news media and the public.

Tony Stewart says he became a champion stock car driver by playing countless hours of video games when he was young.

"I could play for five hours at a time," Stewart said in 2005 at the annual season-ending jamboree in New York. The same reflexes Stewart honed with a flick of his fingers now serve him well making left turns at 175 miles an hour. "I didn't like fighting and war games, but I liked puzzle games," he said.

Stewart's father, Nelson Stewart, was a racer, and raised him to be competitive. For a while, Stewart drove a tow truck, and he envisioned himself as a construction worker. Stewart drove anything with wheels, and he wound up on the Joe Gibbs Racing Team, where he acquired a reputation for having a temper. It is often written that Stewart sought "anger management," but J. D. Gibbs, the team president and son of the owner, said it was more like an intervention by crew members that shocked Stewart into realizing his negative impact on other people. "Did he actually go for counseling?" Gibbs said. "Not really. He just had to realize you can't be a complete jerk or you won't have a ride."

Success soon followed. Maybe Stewart's nicer public personality had nothing to do with it, but being a good guy didn't seem to hurt. Where he had been booed during the driver introductions, he was now cheered. Fans wore his T-shirts.

Stewart seemed to think the transformation was funny. If he kept his mouth shut, he won more fans. But the fans realized he was a good driver for a good team, not just a hothead, and he often had interesting things to say.

When he won a race at Indianapolis in August 2005, he jumped out of his car and climbed the catch fence that separates the grandstands from the track. Stewart, from the nearby town of Columbus, Indiana, was overjoyed, and the fans were happy for him.

After winning the Allstate 400 in Indianapolis, Tony Stewart climbs the fence in celebration.

Such contact, even fleeting, keeps the fans coming back. Big race teams set up small boxes in front of their haulers where fans can get free photos of the drivers and their cars. Little touches like that mean a lot.

As a result, the races draw thousands. The two races yearly at Pocono, which is not a particularly big stop on the circuit, draw an estimated 100,000 fans each, even though they are just one month apart.

It is hard to find an empty patch of grandstand at a Nascar Nextel Cup race. The best tickets to a race are not cheap—usually well over a hundred dollars apiece—but anyone who wants to go to a race can find some ticket that fits the family budget. In 2006, an infield ticket at the Pocono Raceway cost about $40, while luxury boxes cost $250.

But despite the large numbers, nearly all of these fans are white. Nascar has worked hard to lure minorities to auto racing, not just as fans but to become drivers and crew members, but without much success.

Nascar fans seem to have their own demographic. During the 2004 election, the Republican Party, seeking to reelect President George W. Bush, was said to be trying to get the votes of so-called Nascar Dads across the country.

A Nascar Dad was thought to be a middle- or working-class white male between the ages of forty and fifty who did not live in a metropolitan area. Securing the votes of enough Nascar Dads was seen as a key to the election.

But there are many more people at a Nascar race than Nascar Dads. Some wear T-shirts of their favorite drivers. Some do not even know the names of more than a couple drivers in the race.

What they all seem to enjoy is the atmosphere. A race is a special gathering place—a place to watch cars and the rest of the world go by. Some fans do not even watch the races; they just enjoy feeling as if they are part of an event. Sometimes that desire to join in can

Air Force One, with President Bush aboard, above the Daytona track in 2004.

lead people to do some pretty strange things.

At a race at Watkins Glen, New York, a fan of Dale Earnhardt Jr. decided that he would make his upper body look like Earnhardt's car, which is red with white numbers and the name of his sponsor, Budweiser, across the hood. The day before the race, he taped a number eight and "Bud" onto his torso. Then he sat in the sun until his skin burned bright pink. He took off the tape, leaving white skin.

Nascar has branched out from its base in the southeastern United States, and with the exception of the Pacific Northwest, there are Nextel Cup races within reasonable driving distances of every major American city.

A few years ago, Nascar drew up plans to build a racetrack on Staten Island in New York City. It has always been encouraged by the steady attendance at Pocono, which is about a hundred miles west of New York, and a presence in the country's largest urban area would be a major statement about the sport's appeal.

How do I cheer on my favorite driver? Let me count the ways!

Nascar likes to say that its biggest races draw more than a Super Bowl, an NBA finals game, and a World Series game combined. Of the twenty sporting events in the United States that drew the largest attendance in 2004, seventeen were Nascar events.

Contrary to their reputation among non-racing fans, stock car fans are not all from the Southeast—or male. According to Nascar, females compose 40 percent of its fan base, even though there have not been many female drivers.

Girls and women like stock car racing for many of the same reasons men and boys do—the speed of the cars and the excitement of the event. They like the rakish yet homespun personalities of the drivers.

I watched Dale Earnhardt Jr. walk through the garage area at the Indianapolis Motor Speedway the August after his father's death. Earnhardt, in his red fire suit, drew a crowd, which quickly grew to around fifty. Several women began to scream as if they had just seen a rock star. Earnhardt seemed unfazed. He was used to it.

Dale Jr. became the most popular Nascar driver not long after his father died. Part of his appeal is his famous last name, of course. But Dale Jr. also quickly became the most eligible bachelor in the series. He is handsome, with a tuft of short reddish hair and sometimes a goatee, and he is also straightforward, brash, and hilarious. Men like him as much as women do, because he seems like a guy who would be fun to hang out with. A fan once asked Dale Jr. to autograph his chest. It would be, the fan said, a permanent tattoo. He told Dale Jr. that he planned to go to a tattoo artist to have a replica of the signature put over the original. Dale Jr. smiled, rolled his eyes, signed the man's chest, and said, "Whatever."

Through the glass, a crowd at Daytona watches Dale Earnhardt Jr. prepare for a race.

Nascar boasts that it has 75 million fans of all ages. One-third of them are between the ages of eighteen to thirty-four. Television viewers in Atlanta are more likely to watch a Nascar broadcast than viewers in any other major American market. Tampa, Florida, is the fifth television market. But New York, Los Angeles, and Philadelphia—all far from the South—were also in the top five.

Nascar fans are known to buy a lot of products from the corporations that sponsor the sport. Drivers are known by sponsors, and sponsors by their drivers. Tony Stewart's orange Chevrolet, for example, has often been identified as "the Home Depot car."

If you go to a Home Depot, part of a nationwide chain of home improvement stores, you might notice soda machines selling Coca-Cola products outside with Stewart's photo on them, because Coke is an associate sponsor of his. Because he often wins or is in contention to win, Stewart provides Home Depot with lots of exposure on telecasts of Nextel Cup races. Stewart, like other drivers, makes sure to mention his sponsor in post-race interviews.

Dale Earnhardt Jr. celebrates a win with Teresa Earnhardt, his stepmother.

Stock cars have been called "rolling billboards," and sometimes not approvingly. Cars appear to be totally covered by corporate logos or stickers. The front left quarter-panels of cars are covered by as many as fifteen to twenty stickers of a car's smaller sponsors.

Many cars are equipped with onboard cameras so viewers can

see what the drivers are doing or what is going on directly in front of them. These cameras usually include the sponsor's logo, positioned so that it appears in the camera image.

Onboard cameras allow viewers to see what the drivers are doing or what is going on directly in front of them.

Even a driver's fire suit is covered with logos, so the names of his sponsors can be seen during interviews on television and in newspaper photographs. After drivers tug off their helmets following races, they often put on baseball caps with logos on them.

There are commercial signs everywhere at a Nextel Cup race. Even the trash cans behind a wall along pit road are lined with yellow plastic covers advertising Nextel products. Nextel, which merged with another communications giant, Sprint, has figured that the money it spends on racing helps business. During the first two years of its sponsorship of the series, the number of customers it had among Nascar fans doubled. Sprint-Nextel officials calculated that the usage of the company's cell phones at Nascar racetracks rose 21 percent between 2004 and 2005.

The Home Depot will not say how much it spends on sponsoring Stewart's car, but the company considers it to be a worthwhile investment. According to Nascar, each Nextel Cup race broadcast on television in 2004 drew an average of nine million viewers.

Nascar has carefully structured its schedule to maximize fan interest, devising "The Chase for the Nextel Cup" in 2004. The ten races of the Chase coincide with the first half of the National Football League season, which has traditionally lured viewers away from stock car races every September.

The first Chase was both exciting and popular. Kurt Busch won

Kurt Busch
takes a victory
lap after winning
the 2004
Nextel Cup.

the title in the closest finish ever, and NBC said that its audience for the final ten races increased by 12 percent. Tickets to the second Chase in 2005 sold quickly.

The same drivers who said in 2004 that they did not like the Chase admitted a year later that it was good for the sport. People paid attention. Stewart appeared for the first time on *The Late Show with David Letterman* in September 2005. "It was another one of those reality checks to show that we've made it to the big time," he said the next day.

Shawna Robinson was told by female fans: "Do it for the girls. Do it for us."

In May 2005, a female rookie Indy car driver named Danica Patrick stole some thunder from Nascar and stock car racing by leading the Indianapolis 500 for a few laps and finishing fourth. She was a sensation.

There have not been many female drivers in Nascar history. At Brooklyn, Michigan, on June 10, 2001, Shawna Robinson, a veteran driver, became the first female driver in twelve years to drive in a Winston Cup race; she finished thirty-fourth.

They thought she wouldn't make it. Once she did, they thought she couldn't finish. Shawna Robinson proved them wrong.

In 2001, she became the first woman to compete in a Winston Cup event in twelve years. Then she became the first woman to finish a race since 1988.

"You have to understand, what every single driver out there expected me to do was probably crash or get in the way," Robinson said. "I think I did neither of those things, so my goal was accomplished."

Robinson started thirty-second and finished thirty-fourth in the Kmart 400—three laps behind the race winner, Jeff Gordon.

But it was the only Winston Cup race she drove in that year. A year later, Robinson drove in seven races, becoming the first woman in twenty years to compete in more than one race in a single season. But she failed to catch what drivers call a "full-time ride"—enough money from a sponsor to fund a full season of racing instead of sporadic races.

I talked to Robinson in her motor home at Talladega not long before she qualified for the race in Michigan. In a polite and even voice, she said that her quest to make the Winston Cup series had been difficult. Men dominated Nascar.

She talked about several female fans coming up to her at the racetrack and saying, "Do it for the girls. Do it for us." Robinson then said, "That's nice, but it's hard, because you want to run well anyway."

Not long after Danica Patrick's race at Indy, Ray Evernham, the Nextel Cup team owner, announced that Erin Crocker, a driver from Massachusetts who had shown talent in the lower levels of racing, would drive a Busch series car full-time for him in 2006.

Evernham had faith in Crocker's ability to develop in a lesser series before plunging her into Nextel Cup racing. Many male drivers, Dale Earnhardt Jr. and Jeff Gordon among them, had taken the same route to the top of the sport.

Crocker was quickly nicknamed "Nascar Danica." Stock car racing surely pulled in a few more fans who would keep up with Crocker's progress on the track. It was another story line in a series already full of them.

Erin Crocker, a driver who had shown talent at lower levels of racing, drove a full-time Busch series car in 2006.

SIX

The Future
"You're Still Driving a Racecar"

Almost a year to the day after Dale Earnhardt was killed, a pleasant sixty-year-old man with gray hair and big glasses strolled into the infield media center at Daytona International Speedway to be interviewed by reporters. His name was Dave Marcis.

He was not a Nascar official, a racetrack executive, or a crew chief. He was a driver. The 2002 Daytona 500 would be his thirty-third and last, and Marcis, who had not won a Winston Cup race in almost twenty years, would be starting fourteenth.

Marcis was his own one-car team, and he said he was retiring because he wanted to run a hunting lodge in his native state of Wisconsin. Every now and then in the news conference he would ask someone to repeat a question because he was hard of hearing.

He won only five of the 883 races he drove in. And as it turned out, his car would sustain engine problems early in this race, and he would finish in forty-first place, two spots out of last.

Marcis seemed to be a throwback from Nascar's past. As a result of a series of driver deaths that included Earnhardt's, Nascar officials had implemented changes that they believed would make racing safer. Even an old-timer like Marcis followed the rules carefully. But his driving uniform included something that I don't recall having seen before or since: a pair of black wingtip dress shoes. I don't think anyone is likely to race a stock car wearing black wingtips again.

It seems quaint now, when drivers wear soft-soled boots. Many even place heat-resistant shells over the heels of their boots so their feet are not burned by the bottom of a hot car during a long race.

Today, strapped tightly to their seats, a restraint device cradling their heads, drivers resemble astronauts in a spaceship. Their thick helmets have shields, and their suits are flame-resistant.

The racetracks' hard concrete walls have been covered in many places by what are called SAFER (steel and foam energy reduction) walls, which reduce the force of impact and as a result have made crashes much less severe.

A statue of Dale Earnhardt was erected in his hometown of Kannapolis, North Carolina, not long after he died. A few miles south, there is another significant monument to Earnhardt.

At a cost to Nascar of $10 million, a 61,000-square-foot research and development center opened December 2002 with a mandate to make racing safer.

The center does not bear Earnhardt's name, but perhaps it should. In some ways, he is responsible for many of the major improvements in racing safety in recent years.

Even before he died, safety concerns had become an issue for Nascar. The series had lost two drivers the year before; Adam Petty and Kenny Irwin died in separate crashes two months apart in 2000.

The research and development center was a significant step for Nascar, which often left safety issues to the drivers and the crews.

Few safety improvements had been made after Petty and Irwin were killed. Nascar was notoriously slow when it came to tinkering with the sport.

That was, until Dale Earnhardt was killed in February 2001. The Earnhardt crash accelerated the pace of change within Nascar, and the ensuing investigation was unprecedented for the sport.

For the first time, Nascar went outside the family and brought in experts to understand and to learn from the crash. Now cars are equipped with crash boxes that collect data, including G-forces, change in speed, impact patterns, and angle of impact, in the event of an accident. Drivers are now required to wear head-and-neck restraints, and some use safer, form-fitted seats made of composite fiber instead of aluminum. Full face shields are recommended. SAFER barriers, which absorb energy in a crash, have been installed at many tracks.

Those who knew Earnhardt Sr. believe Nascar would not have been nearly as aggressive in developing safety equipment had it not been for his death.

But if that is his lasting impact on the sport, it is not how many around Nascar, including his son, want to remember Earnhardt. "I'm sure he would be very proud to know that a lot of improvements have been made," Dale Jr. said. "But I think I want him to be remembered for the races he won, the people that were his fans, how he affected their lives, how he made their Sundays more enjoyable."

Driver Carl Edwards does a ceremonial backflip to celebrate a win.

A sport that attracted fans because it was dangerous is still dangerous, but less so. Crashes can be spectacular, but they tend not to be as catastrophic. Drivers are still injured, but their injuries are often less serious than they used to be.

Edwards believes staying fit provides an edge.

The days when a driver would wear an open-face helmet and goggles as his only protection—one old photo shows Junior Johnson wearing a helmet, goggles, a white T-shirt, and work pants as he got ready to climb into his car—seem so long ago.

Dick Trickle, a former driver, was said to have smoked in his car during caution periods. Nowadays, young drivers like Carl Edwards work out regularly. Edwards figures that staying fit could give him an edge.

Old school: Dick Trickle smoked in his car during caution periods.

Stock car racing has changed in many other ways, and will almost certainly continue to evolve. For one thing, foreign automakers are poised to enter the field and may stoke even more interest. Toyota, a Japanese automaker, entered the Nascar's pickup truck racing series in 2004 and will produce cars for the Nextel Cup and Busch series as early as 2007.

Whether they are made by American or foreign manufacturers, stock cars are bound to go through some radical changes in the future. Much of Nascar's attention has been devoted to what the organization has called the "Car of Tomorrow." The car, a safer but slightly slower version of the current stock cars, was first test-driven late in the 2005 season. It is slightly taller than the average stock car and has a boxier shape. The driver's seat is more toward the center of the car, and its front is designed to meet less wind resistance. It looks more like the front of the trucks that are raced by Nascar, and truck racing has proven to be close and exciting.

Jack Roush owns five of the ten teams that participated in the 2005 Chase for the Nextel Cup.

Nascar plans to introduce the Car of Tomorrow gradually, but some car owners are upset because they have invested so much money in building racecars that follow the old rules and would become obsolete if those rules change.

Along with the Car of Tomorrow, Nascar is also considering limiting the size of the racing teams. Jack Roush owns five of the ten cars that participated in the 2005 Chase for the Nextel Cup, which is contrary to Nascar's preference for competitive balance. Roush's five crews and drivers earned those spots in the Chase, but Nascar doesn't want one competitor to dominate the field, and it is worried that too many big teams would discourage smaller teams from staying in the series. After all, Nascar was built on the hard work of one-car teams.

It's also possible that the technology that fuels stock cars could be different in future years. American automakers formed an alliance with Nascar because they figured that if one of their cars won on a Sunday, more people would come into the showroom on Monday. As automakers sell more and more hybrid fuel cars, there will be a bigger incentive to race them.

But perhaps the biggest change in Nascar's future may be the nature of the events themselves. Now Nascar is as much about the spectacle of the live event as it is about the television coverage. It is always fun to watch the big bleachers slowly fill with thousands of fans. Even an hour before a race, not every seat is filled, and it looks as if the stands will not reach full capacity. But as the drivers are introduced and the national anthem is sung, people find their way to their seats and there does not seem to be an inch of open bleacher space.

As gasoline prices spiraled in 2005, I did notice rows of empty seats at some races.

One family brought their own pool to a Busch series race in Daytona.

Nascar tracks do not release specific attendance figures, only estimates, but it seemed to me as if fewer fans were going to races. Stock car racing is a family-friendly sport, but rising ticket prices, combined with the cost of traveling to a race, might prove to be too much for some families. That, along with better television coverage, may change the way that people watch Nascar races.

There are an estimated four thousand American kids, ages five to thirteen, in quarter-midget racing, driving fiberglass racers with 2.5- to 4-horsepower engines that can reach speeds of almost forty miles an hour. Some go on to race late-model cars at fourteen, modified pickup trucks at sixteen, Winston Cup at eighteen, or even Indy cars and Formula One. This may be the future of American auto racing in the same way that Little League became the Head Start program for American-born baseball players. Such Nascar headliners as Jeff Gordon, Tony Stewart, and the Labonte brothers, Terry and Bobby, started out strapped into these snarling machines, caged by padded roll bars, supported by pit parents.

"It's the biggest family sport you will see," said Bonnie Henry, the self-described "pit mom" of a twelve-year-old racer. "I call football and baseball the 'drop-off sports,' because parents leave their kids at the field and drive away. We know where our kids are and who they're with because we're here, too," Henry said. "They learn sportsmanship and valuable morals. We meet other families. The rewards are high."

So are the costs: about five thousand dollars to start and at least several hundred a month for fuel and repairs, not to mention travel and time spent.

Television ratings are rising, especially for races during prime time, and Nascar would like to stage more Nextel Cup races at night. Night racing leads to long days and late nights for fans, who might prefer to stay home and watch the race on TV.

Saturday-night racing on small, short tracks is as important to stock car racing as the Nextel Cup. The stars of the future learn how to race on these area tracks. But would fans come to watch them if there was a Nextel Cup race on television?

Some question whether Nascar's season schedule is too long. The Nascar season, a full nine months, runs from February to November. The major-league baseball season starts in April and ends in October, only seven months.

In 1973, shortly after Nascar's top series was named the Winston Cup, there were only twenty-eight races on the schedule. The length of the season was about the same as now, but there were more breaks in the schedule—and each race meant a little bit more.

Night racing, long a staple of the minor circuits, may be going big time.

It is difficult to eliminate races, because most of them draw big crowds. Joseph Mattioli, the owner of Pocono Raceway, a track that drivers seem to either love or hate, told me that Big Bill France promised him that Pocono would always have two annual races. To add races in new venues, Nascar dropped them at some of the small tracks that were part of its early heritage—including the track near Junior Johnson's home in North Wilkesboro, North Carolina, and the one in Rockingham, North Carolina, at which Steve Park won a race eight days after Dale Earnhardt's death.

The top drivers cannot afford to skip races, because they would lose championship points and prize money. Paring the schedule to thirty races would make the season less of a grind and more exciting for the competitors and fans.

One idea that was seriously considered for a while was the creation of two parallel series, like the National and American leagues in baseball. The drivers in each series would run, say, twenty-four races, with a series of playoff races, like the current Chase, determining a champion. The idea seems to have been shelved for now, but like anything else in Nascar, that is always subject to change.

Rusty Wallace, shown here in 1984, was a rare non-southern champion when he took the season trophy in 1989.

Such changes may help Nascar broaden its appeal and change its image as a strictly southern sport. The good ol' boys of the southeastern United States were the first heroes of stock car racing. And for a long time they were just about the only heroes. From 1949 through 1991, all but three series

champions were born in the South. (The exceptions? Bill Rexford, born in Conowango Valley, New York, was the 1960 champion; Benny Parsons, born in Detroit, won in 1973; and Rusty Wallace, from St. Louis, won in 1989.)

When Alan Kulwicki, from Greenfield, Wisconsin, won the 1992 championship, he was regarded as an outsider. Then other drivers from non-southern states, most notably Jeff Gordon, who was born

Jeff Gordon's number 24 racecar after winning a race in 1994.

in California and raised in Indiana, won championships, too.

But there have been no champions of color, no champions born outside the United States, and no female champions. Nascar has tried to develop interest in its sport everywhere, but its history seems to be a formidable hurdle.

"We want our sport to look more like America," Nascar chief executive officer Brian France, Big Bill France's grandson, said in a Nascar news release in 2005. Nascar formed a diversity council in 2000 and launched a "Drive for Diversity" program that seeks to develop women and minority drivers and crew members. It supports an urban racing school based in Philadelphia for aspiring minority drivers. The Busch series held its first race in Mexico in March 2005 and launched a regional racing series in Mexico in 2006. Nascar plans to promote races at basketball games and concerts.

Nascar has also celebrated the end of each season in New York City since 1982 with a week of activities in early December. At the end of the 2005 season, Nascar drivers teased New Yorkers—who did not have a race of their own—with a so-called Victory Lap. A parade of the top ten cars began at Rockefeller Center, then cruised through Times Square, which had been blocked off from traffic during a normally busy weekday morning.

The lap drew big crowds. The drivers were supposed to drive slowly, but they became competitive—just as they are on the racetrack. They got carried away and began to do smoke-raising burnouts, spinning their tires to burn the rubber, along the route. The crowd wanted more.

Jeremy Mayfield said that a businessman along the route, briefcase in hand, pointed to him and spun his index finger—a burnout request. So Mayfield did a roaring burnout. Ryan Newman surprised the crowd, and apparently the New York Police Department, by turning a burnout into a full spinout—swinging his car into a

In the limelight: A pace car leads Nascar drivers through New York City's Times Square in 2005.

rotating skid. Nascar can turn even a parade into The Show.

The New York events, along with the potential new track in Staten Island, may be the beginning of the end of Nascar's reputation as a strictly southern sport. But the organization still has big hurdles to get over before it becomes truly diverse.

Flags flown by a fan at the Darlington raceway.

Until only recently, it was common to see Confederate flags flying over the campers of some fans, and only one black driver has won a race in Nascar's top series: Wendell Scott at Jacksonville, Florida, in December 1963. Scott, a former taxi driver from Virginia, was sixth in the Grand National standings in 1966.

A few African Americans have competed since Scott. The most notable is Bill Lester, a former sports car racer who joined the Nascar Craftsman Truck series in 2000 and became a competitive driver.

Some foreign drivers are beginning to notice stock car racing as well. I talked to Klaus Graf, who grew up in the Black Forest section of Germany but was hoping to make a career as a Nascar driver. He had driven just about every kind of racecar there was, but the popularity of Nascar appealed to him.

He grew up, as most Europeans do, as a fan of Formula One, a worldwide series of races in cars that look similar to those driven in the Indianapolis 500. Formula One racing has long been considered as the most elite series in the world.

"Right now, in my opinion, Nascar Nextel Cup, besides Formula One, is the most popular form of racing in the world," Graf said in 2004. "It's just a matter of adjusting. At the end of the day, you're still driving a racecar with four wheels and a steering wheel."

Bill Lester:
A former sports car racer who joined the Nascar Crafts-man Truck series in 2000.

Drivers from other series have occasionally tried Nascar. The great racecar driver Mario Andretti won the 1967 Daytona 500. A. J. Foyt, a four-time winner of the Indianapolis 500, won seven races in Nascar's top series.

It would be interesting to see more established Nascar stars try other forms of racing. But drivers' schedules are so packed with racing, practicing, testing, and fulfilling sponsor obligations that there is little time left for other endeavors.

A. J. Foyt: Four-time winner of the Indianapolis 500.

Sometimes I think drivers spend as much time talking to the news media—television, newspapers, Internet sites, and radio—as they do driving. I remember a humid August afternoon in Watkins Glen, New York. It was Friday, the day in which drivers take their cars out for practice. But the skies turned dark and the wind picked up. A sprinkle of rain suddenly became a downpour and practice was stopped.

In his garage area, Jeff Gordon hopped out of his Chevrolet and talked for a while with Robbie Loomis, who was then his crew chief.

About a hundred feet away, a dozen or so reporters huddled under the overhang of Gordon's trailer. Rain was pounding the racetrack, and the overhang began to leak. The reporters started to get wet.

Gordon, smiling, walked over and began to answer questions. The reporters got soaked, scratching his quotes onto their rain-blotched notepads. Gordon's team was struggling; it would not make the 2005 Chase, and Loomis would soon be replaced. But Gordon answered every question, looking the reporter who asked it straight in the eye.

Though Gordon sets aside a period after every Friday practice to answer questions, this impromptu session said a lot about Nascar's openness. Even though he was not doing well, Gordon was still willing to talk about his car and his season. Not every professional athlete is so engaging.

That may be why Nascar racing, whatever changes may come down the line, will continue to be one of the most popular sports in the country. However many races it runs every season, and no matter what the cars look like, Nascar is big business, and it will probably continue to be for years to come.

According to Nascar, stock car racing now counts 75 million fans—more than a quarter of the United States' population—and more than the entire populations of Britain, France, and Iran. Nascar's TV deals alone are worth $2.8 billion, and its licensed-product sales are worth another $2 billion annually.

One year, a week before Halloween, I went to a Target store in New Jersey to look at the displays of spooky costumes and decorations. The store had already placed a Christmas display in the middle of the Halloween items for sale.

Everything in the display was Nascar related. There were red Christmas tree balls with a familiar white slanting number 8—Dale

Factory workers in Macao paint toy stock cars.

Earnhardt Jr.'s number. There were ornaments that looked like Jeff Gordon and his number 24 car.

There were also six-inch Santa Clauses dressed in the colors worn by Gordon, Tony Stewart, and Earnhardt.

Nascar rides a gigantic wave of popularity. Would it have become as popular had Dale Earnhardt climbed out of his car after crashing in the 2001 Daytona 500?

It is a question without an answer, of course, because Earnhardt did not climb out of his car and walk briskly back to the garages, a smile cutting through his push-broom mustache. Nascar's big television contracts with Fox and NBC were already in place when Earnhardt died, and the schedule had been expanded. Dale Jr. was already a rising star, and the other Young Guns were on their way.

I think Earnhardt would have driven for only another two or three years. It seemed as if he wanted to make one more strong push for an eighth championship. Had he won it, or come close, I believe he would have retired.

Dale Earnhardt's competitive fire always burned brightly.

He raced because he loved it, but he continued because he knew he was still competitive. Richard Petty drove for eight years after his two hundredth and final victory, and some fans began to feel sorry for him. To the end, Earnhardt's fire burned brightly. Many believe Earnhardt was actually trying to prevent other drivers from passing Michael Waltrip when he was sent into the wall at Daytona.

Seven months before he died, Earnhardt sat in his trailer

at Daytona and told a group of reporters, "If someone tells you I'm riding my years out, they're not paying attention."

He finished second to Bobby Labonte in the points standings in 2000, his last full Nascar season, and he was running at the front of the pack the following year when he was killed. For the rest of the 2001 season, fans rose for the third lap of every race and held three fingers aloft in memory of Earnhardt and his black number 3 car, and the drivers held their positions in the field. It was a nice tribute, but Earnhardt would probably have hated it.

A race was a race to him, and holding anything back was unthinkable. That was the way his predecessors raced. Until the moment he died, literally, Earnhardt was upholding a tradition.

Since then, Nascar racing has become a nation's sensation, and there is really no telling where it will stop. Maybe that is why so many people have hopped onto the souped-up bandwagon to see the latest developments. Stock car racing always seems to offer one more thrill. And as long as there are thrills, The Show will go on.

Dale Earnhardt Jr. performs a 360-degree spin known as a "donut."

Source Notes

The following articles were excerpted as text boxes:

1: February 18, 2001
p. 15: Lipsyte, Robert. "Earnhardt's Death Turns Nascar Talk to Safety." *The New York Times*, February 20, 2001.

p. 22: Bernstein, Viv. "In Nascar Numerology, No. 3 Means Earnhardt." *The New York Times*, June 5, 2005.

2. The Basics
p. 28: Nobles, Charlie. "At Talladega, Expect Speed, Patience, Nerve (and Rain?)" *The New York Times*, April 15, 2000.

p. 34: Bernstein, Viv. "No Back-Seat Driving for This Big Family." *The New York Times*, November 14, 2004.

p. 36: Bernstein, Viv. "Stewart Poised to Head onto Road Less Traveled." *The New York Times*, November 20, 2005.

3. Technology
p. 41: Bernstein, Viv. "A Crew Chief Is Pushing Buttons and the Envelope." *The New York Times*, October 2, 2005.

p. 47: Huler, Scott. "Anatomy of a Wreck." *The New York Times*, November 19, 2000.

p. 56: Potter, Steve. "Auto Crews Play a Key Role." *The New York Times*, July 24, 1983.

p. 58: Glier, Ray. "Engines Take a Beating at Atlanta Speedway." *The New York Times*, October 30, 2005.

4. History
p. 63: Radosta, John S. "Moon Shining Bright on Stock Cars." *The New York Times*, June 11, 1969.

p. 68: Blunk, Frank M. "Tilting All Machines." *The New York Times*, November 11, 1959.

5. The Fans
p. 83: Caldwell, Dave.

"For Nextel Cup Drivers, There's Just No Point, or Points, to Holding on to Grudges." *The New York Times*, May 1, 2005.

p. 84: Vecsey, George. "For Stewart It's Fun and (Video) Games." *The New York Times*, December 1, 2005.

p. 93: "Woman Finishes Winston Cup Race." *The New York Times*, June 11, 2001.

6. The Future
p. 97: Bernstein, Viv. "Safety May Be the Intimidator's Legacy." *The New York Times*, June 1, 2003.

p. 102: Lipsyte, Robert. "Good Instincts Give Rise to the 'Little Intimidator.'" *The New York Times*, March 11, 2001.

p. 111: Miles, Jonathan. "'Sunday Money' and 'Full Throttle.'" *The New York Times*, May 22, 2005.

Further Reading

To learn more about some of the subjects covered in this book, you may want to read the following articles from *The New York Times*:

Bending the Rules

Bernstein, Viv. "In Nascar, Rules Are for Bending." *The New York Times,* February 21, 2006.

Lipsyte, Robert. "In the Garage, the Race Is Always to Beat the System." *The New York Times,* November 10, 2002.

Radosta, John S. "Cheating in Stock Car Racing Is a Way to 'Stay Competitive.'" *The New York Times,* May 7, 1972.

Radosta, John S. "Crew Pulls Off a Neat Switch, Then Allison Gets Caught in It." *The New York Times,* March 15, 1972.

Car of Tomorrow

Bernstein, Viv. "This Is the Dawn of the Racecar of Tomorrow." *The New York Times,* March 3, 2006.

Diversity

Bernstein, Viv. "Nascar Goes Beyond Roots, and Southerners See Betrayal." *The New York Times,* August 31, 2003.

Bernstein, Viv. "Nascar Looks Past White Male Roots." *The New York Times,* January 7, 2004.

Driving a Stock Car

Lipsyte, Robert. "A First Ride in a Stock Car Unites Man, Speed, and Fantasy." *The New York Times,* January 14, 2001.

Lipsyte, Robert. "Getting Behind the Wheel, Feeding a Soon Insatiable Desire." *The New York Times,* June 3, 2001.

Earnhardt, Dale

Caldwell, Dave. "As the Racing World Grieves, It Also Goes On." *The New York Times,* February 20, 2001.

Caldwell, Dave. "Dale Earnhardt, 49, Racing Star." *The New York Times,* February 19, 2001.

Caldwell, Dave, "Tributes Are Expressed by Fans of All Ages." *The New York Times,* February 20, 2001.

Lipsyte, Robert. "Stock Car Star Killed on Last Lap of Daytona 500." *The New York Times,* February 19, 2001.

Lipsyte, Robert. "Window into America's Hottest New Reality Show." *The New York Times,* February 26, 2001.

Earnhardt, Dale Jr.

Bernstein, Viv. "Earnhardt's Bright Future, and an Un-avoidable Past." *The New York Times,* April 27, 2004.

Bernstein, Viv. "Father's Legacy Inspires Earn-hardt Jr." *The New York Times,* February 16, 2004.

Foreign Automakers
Bernstein, Viv. "World of Change Is Likely as Nascar Lets Toyota Join." *The New York Times,* January 24, 2006.

The France Family
Lipsyte, Robert. "Earnhardt Jr. Helps Nascar Find Its Way Back." *The New York Times,* July 15, 2001.

Siano, Joseph. "How Nascar's Power Figure Keeps Everybody Happy." *The New York Times,* October 20, 1999.

Fuel
Bernstein, Viv. "Nascar Plans to Switch to Unleaded Fuel in '08." *The New York Times,* January 20, 2006.

Bernstein, Viv. "Nascar Unable to Get the Lead Out." *The New York Times,* July 10, 2005.

Bernstein, Viv. "To Gain an Edge in Fuel Use, Newman Says, Do the

Math." *The New York Times,* January 20, 2006.

Gordon, Jeff
Lipsyte, Robert. "Jeff Gordon Does Not Fit Fans' Image." *The New York Times,* November 18, 2001.

Sack, Kevin, "He's Good, He's Golden, and Fans Can't Stand It." *The New York Times,* October 16, 1997.

Siano, Joseph. "Gordon Goes All Out and Finishes in Style." *The New York Times,* December 10, 1995.

Point System
Bernstein, Viv. "Victories Don't Add Up in Nascar Points Chase." *The New York Times,* November 16, 2004.

Rousch, Jack
Bernstein, Viv. "Auto Racing: It Took Time to Reach the Top, but Rousch Intends to Stay." *The New York Times,* February 19, 2006.

Safety
Bernstein, Viv. "Air Purifying Devices Near Nascar Approval." *The New York Times,* May 16, 2003.

Bernstein, Viv. "A Driver's Long Way Back." *The New York Times,* May 16, 2004.

Bernstein, Viv. "Lately, Bumping Is Racing, and Some Say That's Reckless." *The New York Times,* February 16, 2006.

Bernstein, Viv. "Nascar Bumper Cars: It's Fun Until Someone Is Hurt." *The New York Times,* April 10, 2005.

Sponsorship/ Marketing
Bernstein, Viv. "Good Looks and Good Driver Join to Complete a Nascar Package." *The New York Times,* April 15, 2005.

Bernstein, Viv. "Nascar Knows Logos Make Wheels Go 'Round.'" *The New York Times,* June 19, 2005.

Lipsyte, Robert. "Success on Track Leads to Sales in the Showroom." *The New York Times,* June 10, 2001

Neil, Dan. "Chevrolet Monte Carlo SS: A Moving Tribute to a Racing Legend." *The New York Times,* March 3, 2002.

Stock Car Racing in the Past
Radosta, John. "Stock Car Streaking." *The New York Times,* June 16, 1974.

Teamwork
Bernstein, Viv. "Auto Racing: Small Teams Squeezed to Side of Road." *The New York Times,* March 26, 2006.

Huler, Scott. "In Nascar, the Deals Are Short-Lived but the Memories Last Long." *The New York Times,* June 25, 2000.

Lipsyte, Robert. "There's More to Racing Than Driving a Fast Car." *The New York Times,* April 19, 2001.

Tony Stewart
Bernstein, Viv. "Going Home Puts Stewart on Right Track." *The New York Times,* August 7, 2005.

Young Racers
Lipsyte, Robert. "A Teenage Driver Learning to Be Safe at Any Speed." *The New York Times,* June 29, 2003.

Acknowledgments

I discovered that writing a book about Nascar is kind of like driving in the Daytona 500. There is a whole lot of ground to cover, and one person cannot get to the finish line by himself. I am grateful that I have had a race team of my own behind me.

Deirdre Langeland of Kingfisher Publications and Alex Ward of *The New York Times* were my editors for this project. They made so many wonderful suggestions that helped make the book better. Both made writing such a book enjoyable.

Neil Amdur, the classy and knowledgeable former sports editor at *The Times*, suggested to Alex that I write this book. Neil gave me my first assignment for *The Times* in 2000: the Pepsi 400 on July Fourth weekend at Daytona. He let me take it from there. Neil and two former assistant sports editors, Kathleen McElroy and Jill Agostino, artfully steered me through the week that followed Dale Earnhardt's death in 2001. I don't think I would have been able to write Chapter 1 of this book without them.

Robert Lipsyte, a titan of sports journalism, was covering the race for *The Times* from the press box that fateful Sunday at Daytona. Bob became a valuable person to hit up with ideas the rest of the 2001 season—a season that really changed everything.

Jim Hunter and Herb Branham and their staff at Nascar headquarters helped me rustle up facts and figures for this book. Jon Edwards, Mike Arning, Tom Roberts, and Denny Darnell are top-notch public relations representatives for their drivers.

Nascar is no longer as intimate as it was, but it has lots of interesting people to talk to, such as Richard Petty, Dale Earnhardt Jr., Jeff Gordon, Darrell and Michael Waltrip, Ricky Rudd, and Dr. Joseph Mattioli. I miss Dale Earnhardt Sr. He was fun.

Being able to bounce ideas off other writers always helps

a reporter develop knowledge of a sport. Bill Fleischman of the *Philadelphia Daily News* and Monte Dutton of the *Gaston (S.C.) Gazette,* always had time to listen to my (dumb) questions.

I have had a lot of mentors along the way, beginning with Bill Fisher, the former sports editor of the *Lancaster (Pa.) Sunday News*. David Tucker, one of my sports editors at the *Philadelphia Inquirer*, taught me that writing could be tight and full of flair.

While attending the University of Michigan on a fellowship in 1993–94, I was lucky enough to audit a creative writing course taught by Nicholas Delbanco, who helped me be unafraid to cross the Rubicon, as it were, of a book project.

My mother, Audrey Caldwell, has been unflagging in her love and support. My sons, Ben and Danny, gave me space. My unofficial adviser was the gorgeous Dena Daniel, who never thought she would become such a big Fatback McSwain fan.

Picture Credits

The publisher would like to thank the following for permission to reproduce their material. Every care has been taken to trace copyright holders. However, if there have been unintentional omissions, we apologize and will, if informed, endeavor to make corrections in any future edition.

Cover: Jamie Squire/Getty Images; Pages 2–6: George Tiedemann/GT Images; 8: AP/Empics; 10: David Madison/NewSport/Corbis; 11: Mark Wallheiser/Reuters/Corbis; 12: Joe Skipper/Reuters/Corbis; 13: AP/Empics; 14: Chris O'Meara/AP; 16: John D. Simmons/Sygma/Corbis; 17: Jeff Siner/Corbis; 19: Tami Chapell/Reuters/Corbis; 20: Michael Kim/Corbis; 21: Chuck Burton/AP; 23: AP/Empics; 24–25: George Tiedemann/GT Images; 26–27: David Madison/NewSport/Corbis; 29: George Tiedemann/NewSport/Corbis; 30: L. M. Otero/AP; 31–35: George Tiedemann/GT Images; 37: AP; 39: Paul Kizzle/AP; 40: George Tiedemann/GT Images; 42: AP/Empics; 44: Robert E. Klein/AP; 45: Carolyn Kaster/AP; 46–49: George Tiedemann/GT Images; 50: Sam Sharpe/Corbis; 51–52: George Tiedemann/GT Images; 53: Chris Keane/*The New York Times*; 54: Rusty Jarrett/Getty Images; 55: John Russell/AP; 56: Carolyn Kaster/AP; 59: George Tiedemann/GT Images; 60–61: Icon SMI/Corbis; 62: Wade Payne/AP, bottom: Bettmann/Corbis; 63: AP/Empics; 65: Bettmann/Corbis; 66–68: AP; 69: Hulton/Getty; 70–71: Bettmann/Corbis; 72: George Tiedemann/GT Images; 73: David Madison/NewSport/Corbis; 74: Mike Okoniewski/AP/Empics; 75–79: George Tiedemann/GT Images; 81: George Tiedemann/NewSport/Corbis; 82: both by George Tiedemann/GT Images; 85: Chuck Robinson/AP; 86: Michael Kim/Corbis; 87: Roy Dabner/AP; 88: Brian Cleary/AP; 89–90: George Tiedemann/NewSport/Corbis; 91–92: George Tiedemann/GT Images; 94–95: Charlie Neibergall/AP; 97: Erik Perel/AP; 98: Sam Sharpe/Corbis; 99 (top to bottom): George Tiedemann/GT Images, Reuters/Corbis; 100: George Tiedemann/GT Images; 101: David Ferrell/Reuters/Corbis; 103: Erik Perel/Icon SMI/Corbis; 104–5: George Tiedemann/GT Images; 107: Richard Drew/AP; 108: Lou Krasky/AP; 109: George Tiedemann/GT Images; 110–11(top to bottom): AP, George Tiedemann/GT Images; 112: Macduff Everton/Corbis; 113: Winston Luzier/Reuters/Corbis; 114–15: Michael Kim/Corbis; back cover: Gavin Lawrence/Getty Images.

Index

Twenty-One Drivers Race in Coast Event Today *April 15, 1934* • Racing Car Le
on Turn Fatal to Pit Employee at Lockport Track *July 5, 1950* • 500-Mile Stoc
Drivers Injured in Three Accidents at Langhorne *October 15, 1951* • Bluebi
Baseball Compete in Dullness Derby on Video Saturday Nights *May 26, 1952*
October 8, 1952 • Seven Auto Drivers Hurt on Ohio Tracks *October 13, 1*
Developments to Come *December 21, 1952* • Baker Drives to Victory: Avera
Racing Attendance at 23,000,000 for 1953 *January 10, 1954* • Stock Car
1954 • 4-Car Crash in Race Sends 6 to Hospital *February 27, 1955* • Leade
Race Track: Speedway to Be Built for Competitions Formerly Held on the Sho
160.175 MPH in Florida *February 5, 1957* • Flagging Them Off: Daytona Bea
• Nascar Head Runs Daytona Beach Show with Radio-Telephone Network *Febr*
Event *July 7, 1957* • Woman Will Drive Daytona Pace Car *January 29, 195*
Will Be Ready in 1959 *September 17, 1958* • Teague Is Killed in Auto Crash
Hour Lap in Test Run *February 12, 1959* • Fire Razes Grandstand, but 3,0C
Driver Was 26 *May 18, 1959* • World's Noisiest Sport Draws 20,230 of Wor
of 140 MPH at Daytona Is Fastest Time in Class *July 5, 1959* • 3 Killed at 1
Driver Will Try Daytona's Heavily Banked Speedway *November 11, 1959* • Da
Stock Car Race? It's Not in Stock *April 14, 1963* • Stock Car Betters 170 M
Hemispherical Heads Sanctioned for '66 *February 13, 1965* • Ford Will En
December 14, 1965 • 24-Hour Auto Race Scheduled at Daytona Speedway on
Drivers *January 4, 1969* • Daytona Speedway: Fastest in the World for Stock
Stock Drivers Rally and Form Association to Give Them Voice *August 24, 196*
April 5, 1970 • Ford Sets Off a Scramble for Race-Team Sponsors *Novembe*
14, 1971 • Big Purses Await Auto Race Winners *February 21, 1971* • Dirt-1
Season Is Getting to Be Endless Summer *September 13, 1971* • Mr. Nascar
"Stay Competitive" *May 7, 1972* • Nascar Tinkers Again with Carburetor Rule
12, 1975 • Daytona Beach: Tumult and Shouting *February 15, 1976* • Petty
13, 1985 • New Rule to Slow Cars *May 26, 1985* • Has Auto Racing Becor
1991 • The Sport That Roars *May 24, 1991* • William France Is Dead at 8
Crashing Halt *November 16, 1992* • Fatal Crashes Raise Questions of Safety
• He's Good, He's Golden, and Fans Can't Stand It *October 16, 1997* • France
Hero, the Villain Treatment *June 21, 1998* • Big-Budgeted Campaigns for A
Winston Cup: All White at the Wheel *October 20, 1999* • How Nascar's Pc
Family Patriarch, Dies *April 7, 2000* • Youngest Racer of Petty Family Killed i
2000 • France Steps Down as Nascar President *November 29, 2000* • Stock
Leaves Hole in Heart of His Hometown *February 21, 2001* • After Earnhardt
Restrictions *April 25, 2001* • Woman Finishes Winston Cup Race *June 11,*
Releases Report on Earnhardt's Death *August 22, 2001* • What They Didn'
Systems *October 18, 2001* • Nascar Sets Age Requirement *December 14,*
30, 2001 • One Year Later, Nascar's Discovery Rolls On *February 7, 2002* •
and a Commitment to Nascar Sponsors Attract Marketers *July 14, 2003* • Na
for Ranking Drivers *January 21, 2004* • Staten Island: Start Your Engines, N
3, 2004 • Nascar Wasn't Broke, but They Fixed It *September 14, 2004* • To
28, 2004 • For Nascar, Playoff Gamble Wins Big *November 21, 2004* • Reco
Stars Over the Border *March 6, 2005* • Latest Aerodynamics Changes Are
Is in Overdrive *June 26, 2005* • Drivers Fined by Nascar After a Burst
TNT-NBC *October 15, 2005* • Nascar Drives Big Ratings to the Bank